Bertha's Daughters:

A History of the Church in Kent

LINDSAY LLEWELLYN

Copyright © 2021 Lindsay Llewellyn-MacDuff
2nd edition published 2022
All rights reserved.
ISBN: 9798805129309

Acknowledgements

Particular help has been given to me for this project by:
 The sisters of Malling Abbey.
 The Finding Eanswythe project who worked hard to acquaint me with the Anglo-Saxon world, especially the Canterbury Archaeological Trust, who did the heavy lifting with the timeline and the Kentish Royals' family tree.
 Rochester Diocese, and Bishop James in particular, who gave me the space to write this up.
 Rochester Cathedral, with Dr Chris Monk, for much wisdom on their wall mural and on the Textus Roffensis.

Many individuals have also helped me with this project, but it would not have got off the ground without Pamela Ive and her passion for Isabella Gilmore. As for the rest of you — you know who you are — who have encouraged and led me on, my thanks.

Foreword

Preparing (at the time of writing) to receive a refugee family from Ukraine, I realised how little I knew about that country including the reasons behind the current dreadful circumstances there. So I began reading and discovered a fascinating – and at times turbulent and brutal – story of people and places. This story goes back over a thousand years; and it very clearly continues to resonate today and to shape current politics and culture, the lives and the tragic deaths of those in Ukraine today. And faith-related stories are central to that in both negative and positive ways.

If we are to live well in the present, we need to understand something of the past which shapes that present. And stories of people and places are often key to that understanding.

In *Bertha's Daughters*, Lindsay Llewellyn opens up the stories of some of the people who have shaped the life of communities and places in Kent over many centuries, from the earliest years of Christian presence in the area up into the last century. For much of the period when I served as Bishop of Rochester, Lindsay was my Chaplain. In that role, she lived a somewhat peripatetic life as she and I journeyed around the parishes and communities of the Diocese of Rochester which I was visiting in the course of my ministry. And thus Lindsay has added an awareness of West Kent to that which she already had of East Kent.

Perhaps paradoxically, the reading of maps (certainly the following of them) is not Lindsay's strongest suit; but her ear for stories and eye for places has led her to lay out for us a different kind of map. This is a map of people, specifically the women – Bertha's daughters - whom we can recognise as being among the Holy Ones of God. And the lives of these women are intertwined with the stories of the places where they have been – places which have shaped them and which they in turn have shaped. And around the county – and Lindsay would point them out to me –

are to be found physical reminders of these people in those places. Some, such as gravestones, are obvious things to look for; others, such as wells or trees or benches, may be less so. As we go to these places, accompanied by our 'map', so we may have the sense of walking in the steps of others. These women of the past may come to shape our present.

As this book emerged, Lindsay sometimes 'loaned' material to me which would find its way into a sermon delivered on a relevant feast day or at one of the relevant places. And this, I dare to hope, may have allowed something of God to become real for those who heard – the God who is God of past, present and future, and who is glimpsed in the lives of people and places. As *Bertha's Daughters* shares the lives of these holy women with a wider audience, so may it be that more are able to glimpse that which is of God – and hopefully far beyond those with a connection to Kent.

And may it be also that in our wider world, ears for story and eyes for place will lead to lives which are better lived for good and for God.

James Langstaff
Former Bishop of Rochester
Birmingham, April 2022

Contents

Dramatis personae with principal chapter	iv
Dramatis Loci	vi
Kentish Royals, Family Tree	vii
Introduction	1
1: Missionaries	9
2: Pioneers	23
3: Reformers and rebels	43
4: Women in power	61
5: Patrons	73
6: Peacemakers and power-brokers	89
7: Scholars	103
8: Social reformers	121
9: Wives, mothers and daughters	133
10: Virgins	147
Conclusion	163
Thanksgiving for the (Kentish) Holy Ones of God (of Kent)	168
A timeline	171
FOURTH CENTURY	171
FIFTH CENTURY	171
SIXTH CENTURY	172
SEVENTH CENTURY	172
EIGHTH CENTURY	175
NINTH CENTURY	175
TENTH CENTURY	176
LATE TENTH- TO ELEVENTH CENTURIES	177
TWELFTH CENTURY	178

THIRTEENTH CENTURY	179
FOURTEENTH CENTURY	181
FIFTEENTH CENTURY	182
SIXTEENTH CENTURY	183
SEVENTEENTH CENTURY	186
EIGHTEENTH CENTURY	187
NINETEENTH CENTURY	188
TWENTIETH CENTURY	192
TWENTY FIRST CENTURY	195
Glossary	197
a reading list of sorts	202

Illustrations for *Bertha's Daughters* can be found on my Pinterest board *Bertha's Daughters: a History of Kent* -

Scan me for Pinterest Board

including
- Pictures of Sarah Forbes Bonetta
- A Map of Anthony Thorold's Diocese of Rochester
- Bertha's statue in Canterbury,
- Elizabeth Barton's chapel and grove
- An Icon of Elizabeth Barton
- Hilda Stewart's grave and the burial ground at Malling Abbey
- Probably-Goda and the Rochester wall mural
- Octavia Hill's memorial
- 2002 - 2016 £5 note (and the and source picture, which is strikingly different)
- Simone Weil's grave in Ashford

Dramatis personae with principal chapter

Early Kentish
Bertha (St Martin's, Canterbury)	1
Ethelburh (Lyminge)	2
Eanswythe (St Eanswythe's)	10
Domne Eafe (Minster-in-Thanet)	6
Mildburh (Wenlock, Shropshire)	10
Mildthryth (Minster-in-Thanet)	10
Eadburh (Minster-in-Thanet /Lyminge)	2

Post Carolingian Reforms - Pre-Reformation
Wulfthryth of Wilton (Kemsing)	6
Edith of Wilton (Kemsing Well)	7
Countess Goda (Rochester Cathedral)	5
Matilda of Boulogne (Faversham, Dover Castle)	9
Eleanor Plantagenet (Kemsing /Dover Castle)	4
Joan of Kent	9
Joan Burghersh (Canterbury Cathedral)	5

Early Modern
Margery Sandes (Malling Abbey)	5
Joan Bocher (Frittenden /Canterbury)	3
Margaret Roper (Eltham /St Dunstan's Canterbury)	9
Elizabeth Barton (Court-at-Street/ Saint Sepulchre's, Canterbury)	3
Anne Boleyn (Hever Castle)	4
Elizabeth Rede (Malling Abbey)	3
Margery Polley (Pembury)	3
Joan Beach (Tonbridge)	3
Anne Albright, Joan Catmer, Joan Sole, and Agnes Snoth (Canterbury)	3
Pocahontas (Matoaka)/ Rebecca Rolfe (Gravesend)	6

Joanne Bauford and Susan May
    (Faversham and Ashford)   2
Elizabeth Elstob (Canterbury Cathedral)   7
Elizabeth Carter (Deal)   7

Late Modern
Elizabeth Fry (Ramsgate)   8
Harriet/Hilda Stewart OSB (Malling Abbey)   2
Charlotte Boyd (Malling Abbey)   5
Octavia Hill (Crockham Hill)   8
Isabella Gilmore (Gilmore House)   2
Sarah Forbes Bonetta/ Omoba Aina
    (Chatham)   1
Simone Weil (Ashford)   7

Dramatis Loci

Kentish Royals, Family Tree

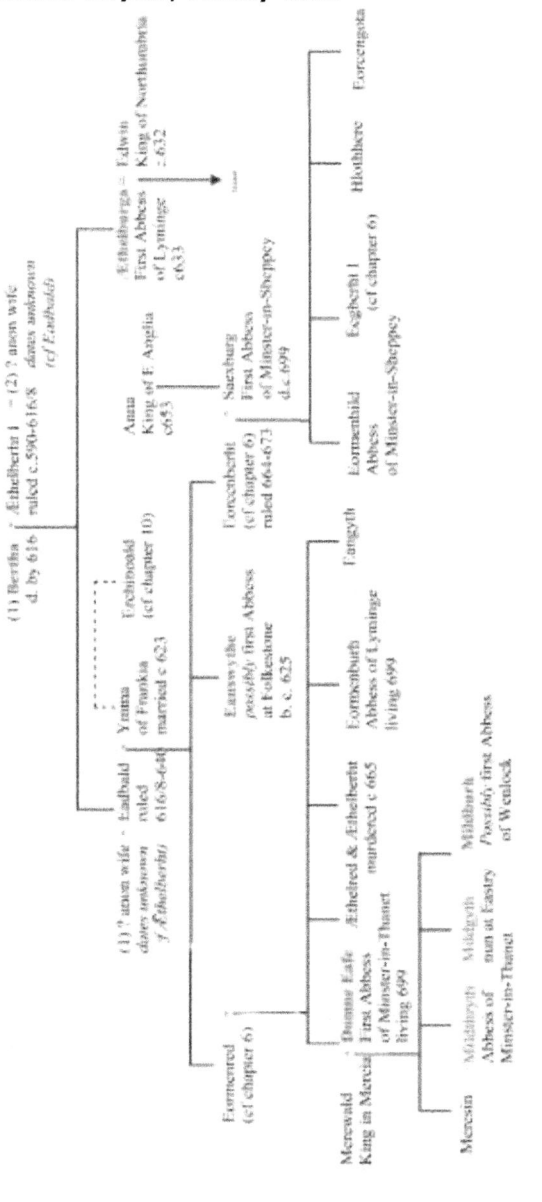

```
                                            (1) Bertha = Æthelberht I = (2) ? upon wife
                                              d. by 616 | ruled c.590-616/8   dates unknown
                                                        |                     (cf Eadbalds)
                        ┌───────────────────────────────┼───────────────────────────────┐
                        |                               |                               |
   (1) ? upon wife = Eadbald          Ymma           Æthelwald              Æthelburga = Edwin
   dates unknown   | ruled         of Frankia       (cf chapter 10)         First Abbess  King of Northumbria
   (cf Æthelberht) | 616/8-640   married c.623                              of Lyminge   +632
                   |                                                        c.633
         ┌─────────┼─────────┐
         |                   |
                         Eanswythe                                Anna      = Saewara
                      possibly first Abbess                    King of E. Anglia   First Abbess
                      at Folkestone                            +653               of Minster-in-Sheppey
                      b. c. 625                                                   d. c. 699
                                                    ┌───────────────┬───────────────┬───────────────┬───────────────┐
                                                    |               |               |               |               |
                                            Eormenburh         Eormenhild        Eorcengota      Ecgberht I      Hlothhere    Eorcengota
                                            Abbess of Lyminge  (cf chapter 6)                    (cf chapter 6)
                                            living 690         ruled 664-673
                                                               Abbess
                                                               of Minster-in-Sheppey

   ┌────────────────┬──────────────────────────┬──────────────────┐
   |                |                          |                  |
Eormenred     Æthelred & Æthelberht        Eormenburh         Eangyth
(cf chapter 6) murdered c.665              Abbess of Lyminge
                                           living 690

Merewald        Domne Eafe
King in Mercia  First Abbess
                of Minster-in-Thanet
                living 690

   ┌────────────┬────────────┬────────────┐
   |            |            |            |
Mercsin    Milburh       Mildgyth       Mildburh
Abbess of  nun at Eastry  Possibly First Abbess
Minster-in-Thanet         of Wenlock
```

vii

Introduction

The origins of this book lie some years ago, when I was trying to persuade my Bishop[1] to give his chapel a dedication. Being an obliging individual, he was content to pursue the idea and suggested I find some worthy local saint. At this distance I can't remember whether it was his idea or mine to narrow the field further and look for a woman. Either way, when I began to look for a holy Kentish woman to be an encouragement for devotion in the chapel, I drew a blank. The only women I could find connected to Kent were a collection of insipid Anglo-Saxon nuns, who seemed to have done very little of any real interest. (The chapel ended up being dedicated to Holy Wisdom.)

There the matter may have rested, had I not had a conversation with a colleague. She sketched out for me the connection of Isabella Gilmore with the Diocese of Rochester, and her significance in the story of the ordination of women. Listening, I was struck by how rich it was with threads of encouragement: for vocations later in life, for vocations among women, for reimagining ministry, for vocations among those with dependents and so on. Out of that conversation there began to form a plan for a festival celebrating Gilmore and women's ministry (somewhat kiboshed by the 2020 pandemic) which this book was intended to resource.

To my surprise, when I started, this time, to set real time aside to look at the contribution that women have made to the life of the Church in this county, I began to find a wealth of material. My search was unlocked when I stopped using 'saint' as the principal search term. Only Gilmore, Fry and Hill have any recognition in the life of the Church of England, although they are not described as 'saints' and are

---

[1] Rt Rev James Langstaff

only minor commemorations. All of the Anglo-Saxon saints herein were removed from the calendar during Cranmer's liturgical reforms, and while one or two of the others are occasionally described as saints in other denominations or traditions, it is never routine.

I'm not arguing that all the women in this book should be described as *saints*, though there are some, I think, that merit the adjective. Nevertheless, they are all women for whom the gospel has had a significant effect on their decisions, and they are all, in one way or another, exemplary. Between them, they give a much more rounded picture of what it means to be both Christian and female, and what is possible under the description. They are all intended to be encouraging.

It's been remarked that "well-behaved women seldom make history."[2] You can find the expression on T-shirts, mugs, even underwear. It is usually deployed as an injunction to women to break the rules, to stand out, to stand up and be noticed. There is also an undertone of disparagement. Well-behaved women, it's implied, will never achieve anything worth writing about. They have toed the line. They are the social equivalents of wage slaves. I often wonder how Laurel Ulrich, who coined the expression, feels when she sees it thus, because it was not written to encourage women to 'misbehave', it was written to encourage historians to look at, *to see* the well-behaved women. These women may not make history, but they do make society. Their invisibility is not because of their insignificance. Just because their lives have not excited the traditional (male) writers of (men's) history, it does not make them irrelevant. It is simply, as Anne Elliott remarks in Jane Austen's *Persuasion,* the natural consequence of men's dominance in society. Her heroine, Anne Elliot, describes the male perspective, and the story of men, as the normative one:

> *"Men have had every advantage of us in telling their own story. Education has been theirs in so*

---

[2] Ulrich, Laurel Thatcher (1976). "Laurel Thatcher Ulrich: Publications: Vertuous Women Found: New England Ministerial Literature, 1668–1735". *American Quarterly*. Harvard University

> *much higher a degree; the pen has been in their hands."*

So let's do something different. Join with me in taking a little time to see what women have done. This is an attempt to populate our imaginations with women who have transformed the church and our understanding of it, who have changed the shape of our country and our society, and who have exercised their faith with enthusiasm, discipline and commitment. This is a population largely absent from the usual description of the church-that-was, which in turn informs our picture of the church-that-is and the church-that-should-be.

It's important because as human beings we think in terms of stories and role models. The more stories we have, the more nuance we can apply in our interpretation of the world around us. The telling of stories shapes our understanding of ourselves and of the people around us. They curtail prejudice — and create it. If we do not have enough different kinds of shape of person in our imagined view of the world then we will only have stereotypes from which to understand people. Then we find ourselves scrunching up the people that we meet to fit in the boxes that we have.[3] This hampers our ability to be for them the person that they need. It also limits our ability to see all the glory of God in creation.

This isn't only altruism. It is very hard to do something that we can't imagine, and it's very hard to imagine something that we haven't seen or heard of. The more examples we have of what it can look like to be a human being, to be a woman, to be a Christian, the more options we have, the more possibilities open up for us. If the world and life of women is unstudied, unseen, unremarkable, then we end up being invisible even to ourselves. This is the repeated refrain of women looking at history, women looking at society, women looking at commerce, at science, at any field you like: that, as the historian Emily Krichbaum says, if you're not part of the information you consume you are less likely to see yourselves as part of the picture.

---

[3] Chimamanda Ngozi Adichie, a Nigerian writer, is very good on this.

And we do not value what we cannot see.[4]

Which means it matters when you open Owen Chadwick's seminal two-volume work on the Victorian church and find not a word on the deaconess movement, and barely three pages on the recovery of women's religious[5] life in Victorian Anglicanism. It matters when you read a book on Anglo-Saxon England and find that the only figures named in key events are the men involved, and the everyday life of women is not described anywhere. It matters when the local history section of a Cathedral library holds one book — *one* — on the life of a woman.

Beyond our history books, it's also in the celebration of our history, too. Of the 29 canons' stalls named after historical people in the Cathedral Quire of Rochester Cathedral, only two are named after women. In the Church of England's liturgical calendar, across the year, there are nearly four times as many men celebrated as women. While the ratio of major feasts: lesser festivals: commemorations among the male saints and worthies is 1:4:4, among the women it is 1:9:16![6] Women are not celebrated in the same numbers, or with the same emphasis as men, and despite the social emphasis on them to be

---

[4] What follows could be described as a short rant. I have tried hard to make this book a positive one, affirming women and women's work, but the imbalance is stark and makes me really quite cross.

[5] Here, 'religious' means either people under religious vows, principally monks and nuns, or an adjective of the same.

[6] *liturgical note:*

I will make several references to the Church of England's calendar of saints, so it's worth including these extracts from Common Worship's *Rules to Order the Christian Year*, by way of explanation (my emphasis).

"The Festivals [aka "red letter days"] ... are not usually displaced. For each day there is full liturgical provision for the Holy Communion and for Morning and Evening Prayer."

"Lesser Festivals, ... are observed at the level appropriate to a particular church. Each is provided with a Collect, Psalm and Readings, which may supersede the Collect of the week and the daily eucharistic lectionary." (Lesser festivals are trumped by red letter days and Sundays.)

"Commemorations ... are made by a mention in prayers of intercession and thanksgiving. They are not provided with Collect, Psalm and Readings, and do not replace the usual weekday provision at either the Holy Communion or Morning and Evening Prayer."

In other words, red letter days are common celebrations of the Church, lesser festivals may affect the tone and theme of the service (as long as nothing more important is happening) and commemorations are by way of a footnote.

communicators and enablers, women are never celebrated as a network of women[7].

Neither do we see many women in our liturgical life. In the Common Worship *Thanksgiving for the Holy Ones of God*, a hymn of praise for the cloud of witnesses,[8] the authors found only four women to celebrate in nearly 1700 years of Christian history in this country, compared to 18 men. Despite recent attempts to modify our language about the community of saints so that it includes women, still the language of our prayers and hymns is full of what men and brothers have done or not done. Whichever side of the argument you land on whether or not the word 'man' really includes women, what it does do is render them invisible. We are absorbed under the umbrella of 'mankind,' absorbed into the masculine narrative, part of the supporting cast of the unnamed and unmentioned ... unimagined.

Then, when we come before God in worship, women are given a comprehensively masculine theophany. I recite that Jesus was "made man"[9] and the other Persons of the Trinity are drawn in almost exclusively male terms. Being in the image of God and conforming to Christ's image begins, liturgically, to look very much like being *male*. God is 'king', 'shepherd', 'potter', not 'queen' or 'weaver' or 'spinster'. Indeed, the Church seems more comfortable using animal metaphors than female ones for God. Count how many more times you encounter 'lion' or 'lamb' or 'eagle', as opposed to, for example, 'mother'.

All this, despite the fact that study after study finds that "globally, women are more devout than men by several standard measures of religious commitment," particularly among Christians (says the Pew Research Centre[10]). How is it of all these women active in the faith, all these women for whom the faith is a significant part of their identity, so few are

---

[7] Unlike the men who are paired up relatively often, suggesting partnership and collaboration, no woman is paired in her festival with other women, but only with spouses and brothers (or, once, unnamed "companions" and once with a sister *and* a brother).

[8] Hebrews 12.1

[9] When the ELLC texts were reviewed by general synod, the more inclusive 'human' was rejected as having too many connotations of fallibility. I'll just leave that there.

[10] *The Gender Gap in Religion Around the World* 2016

remembered, so few have apparently made an impact? How is it that so few of them have been woven into our shared history or feature in our shared language about the Church and the divine?

> *"There's the norm that's the male, and then we've got kind of this subset over here who are not male."*
> *(Helen O'Connell, urologist).*

If women are to identify a vocation outside the invisible sphere of *Kinder, Küche,* (and quietly supporting the) *Kirche*[11] they need a church demonstrating more than masculine language, metaphor and role models. In order to encourage the vocations of the women alongside them, people need to conceive of the things to which they might be called. When the great majority of women's contribution to the life of the church quite literally goes without saying, we are less likely to imagine that the contribution of our sisters, friends and neighbours needs training or support or accreditation.

If the Church is to flourish, to serve God to her fullest capacity, she must have a picture of herself that includes more than half her members. We need to expand a binary view of women, where they are either *extraordinary* — Mother Theresa, say, or Julian of Norwich — or else absorbed into an amorphous mass of good women who populate the church and clean it and feed it without ever being distinguished one from another. The idea that the ordinary woman, the 'well-behaved woman' might be significant in the life of the church requires a leap of imagination on the part of the individual and of the community. That takes a library of examples in our mind's eye, and it takes time to develop and acquire conviction.

Imagine reading history books in which half the stories told were about women. Imagine if half the history told involved subjects and events that concern women. What would it be like if, when we imagine the past, we imagine women, perhaps even as our first examples? This book is an exercise towards that

---

[11] Kinder, Küche, Kirche (Children, Kitchen and Church) is a German expression with origins the nineteenth century, but particularly associated with the Third Reich, denoting the (limited) role of women in society.

project, to place a feather on the balance, the lightest of contributions. This is not 'women's history,' but simply *a* history of the Church in Kent, as contributed to by women. Just like men, women have been scholars, politicians, mediators, rebels, reformers, patrons and missionaries: people who have enriched and altered the church's life, and thus the lives of the people around them.

This is why I wanted to write something focused on their stories, not as extraordinary women but simply as the women who have populated the life of the church in this county with all the wonderful variety of human life. Rather than looking at all the nuns together (which would be rather a long chapter[12]) or all the Anglo-Saxons (ditto), I have put together threads of women as scholars, reformers, patrons and so forth. It does mean that all attempts at chronological order are abandoned, even within a given chapter, but I have provided a timeline for any who would like to know how these women fit together in terms of dates. This approach has created an element of duplication, I'll admit, but hopefully not unbearably so, while giving a better sense of the range of activity involved.

Some may say there has been a degree of cheating, or stretching the definition of 'in Kent' beyond the usual. I don't deny it: not many of the women in these pages have spent their whole life in Kent, nor indeed necessarily much, if any, of their adult life[13], but there is with all of them geographical connection of some kind. A few were born or died here only, some merely passed through, but most were Kentish women / women of Kent.[14] They are all dead. Not because there are no awesome women alive, but it gives the 'vantage of perspective. Nevertheless, I tell their

---

[12] You'd be surprised how many things a nun can do.

[13] In the case of Mildburh (chapter 10), it's not even clear that she was ever in Kent, but she has so many relatives here I let her sneak in. It would have been rude to leave her out.

[14] (Whether you're a Kentish maid or a maid of Kent depends on who you ask. Some place the distinction along the River Medway – west of it and you're a Kentish maid – some say it's a north-south boundary along the river Stour. Others argue that the East-West division is ecclesiastical, and that the maid of Kent is a woman of the Canterbury Diocese. In some versions it's a class boundary, the maids of Kent being better born, in others the Kentish maid is an expat whose parents live *somewhere else in Kent*. However it's reasoned, maids of Kent look down on Kentish maids. This explains a lot.)

stories in the present, because this book is trying to introduce you to them.

None of the people in this book existed in a vacuum. The values of their society, the agency allotted to women of their time and the people around them played a significant part in shaping their lives and witness — as they do for anyone. Some of these women, Domne Eafe, for example, or Isabella Gilmore, were unlikely to have made the impact they did were they not widowed relatively young. On the other hand other women navigated the boundaries set by society and escaped them. Elizabeth Fry and Eleanor Plantagenet were both married with many children without any discernible constraining of their agency despite the expectations of their eras.

More often there are compromises, lives taken off track. Elizabeth Elstob, for example, would have got nowhere without a brother willing and able to support her and a Queen to promote her, and the loss of both of these people in a short span of time signalled the end of her publishing career. Pocahontas would have remained an enterprising, if unrecorded, woman among her own people had she not encountered and helped the European trader John Smith. Thereafter she was integrated into the story of the colonisation of the American subcontinent and her story became about far more than her own life.

Nevertheless, there is hopefully a sense of the fundamental interconnectedness of these women from Bertha[15] to the present day. Many of their stories are accounts of women assisting one another, trying to open the door wider for those who came after or standing on the shoulders of those who came before. In this sense we are, all of us women in Kent, Bertha's daughters.

---

[15] The first Christian woman in Kent that anyone has heard of. (See chapter one.)

Missionaries

From the get-go Christianity has been a proselytising religion. It exploded out of an obscure corner of the Middle East, desperate to explain to the world that the nature of reality had radically changed. It engaged with pagans, Jews, with anyone, in fact, regardless of their desire to listen. So integral to the DNA of Christianity is this drive, that the Church almost seems to become bored and distracted when she is a majority concern. When she can't look outwards, she looks inwards, and that is never good for her. The Church, in other words, only really thrives when there are people around who don't agree.

Women have always been on the front-line of Christian mission. From Lydia and Phoebe in the New Testament through to Perpetua and Monica in the Early Church on to Bertha and Ethelburh in Anglo-Saxon Kent, and then the shadowy Victorian women hidden under their husband's names, women have been missionaries. And good at it.

For starters, they have often had the most to gain from a religion that teaches equality, peacefulness and a radical inclusion of the outsider. It (broadly) eschews those taboos of physicality which have often resulted in women being not only socially but physically excluded, particularly in times of menstruation and childbirth. Perhaps most importantly, it has a habit of encouraging education, which itself invariably leads to emancipation and self-worth. Women have been fertile ground for a gospel of liberation in the name of a man who was as content to teach Mary of Bethany as Nicodemus.

These women, whom Western European society has put in charge of the home, have had natural networks along which to pass the faith. Habitually socialised to be communicators and persuaders, women are usually the glue of their extended family, and in many societies they establish cooperative trading and/or industrial textile networks (cf Lydia, Acts 16). Then there are often additional networks created for the purpose of spreading the word. For example, the (Anglo-Saxon) Frankish Regent, Queen Balthild (a woman of considerable power and influence in the middle of the seventh century) created an international network of female monasticism. From this she seeded the Kentish houses with people, relics and books, often training up Anglo-Saxon young women in her own houses. Similarly, the Victorian missionaries created close associations back in the UK for support and for mustering resources.

It has been in women's domain — the home — that the infant church is gathered, among the domestic staff for whom the matriarch is usually responsible. Rebecca Parker, the 19th century missionary in Travancore, India, wrote of the "great chances for the spread of the gospel by women amongst women..." on account of the unparalleled access that women have to the homes of other women. She said,

> *"Once inside the... apartments of a high-caste house, you have your congregation before you from the grandmother to the latest-born infant of the household. Interest them, show yourself to be their friend, help them in sickness or trouble, and you not only have their gratitude but you may be sure of an attentive hearing for the good news you long to give."*

This has been the key to a great deal of mission through the centuries. It was a key grasped most firmly by the Victorians.

Theirs was a social identity that very much revolved around home and hearth. Young Victorian (middle-class) women were taught that they were fragile creatures who needed to be protected by their fathers until old enough to be handed over to a suitable husband. To him they were to be a helpmeet, an 'angel of the hearth' to bear and tend his children, maintaining a soothing domestic space for him to return to. The segregated society to which they belonged also left men extremely uncertain when faced with the prospect of teaching children or speaking to women to whom they were not related. Women's 'natural maternal instincts' made them, it was assumed, much more fitting missionaries to the domestic sphere and to children. Indeed, even their 'power of conversation' was by some Victorians assumed to give them an advantage in the learning of languages.

Missionary societies, therefore, actively sought out married men to send abroad, often screening the wife as vigorously as the husband. She was a vital model of proper Christian domesticity for the new converts and, it was increasingly perceived, invaluable in the development of girls' education. Into this context walks **Sarah Forbes Bonetta**.

Bonetta is born Omoba Aina to the royal family of the Yoruba people in Nigeria in 1843. Five years later her home is destroyed and her family killed in a local war. The victorious king, Ghezo, is steeped in the slave trade and it's likely this was the purpose of his invasion. He takes the princess captive as the last remnant of the rival Royal family. Here, a slave in Ghezo's court, Princess Aina first meets Capt Frederick Forbes two years later. He had been sent to the Kingdom of Dahomey on a British diplomatic mission to negotiate an end to Ghezo's participation in the Atlantic slave trade. In this he was unsuccessful, the slave trade being an extremely lucrative business for Ghezo. The story goes that Capt Forbes sought to rescue the little girl whom he understood was destined to be sacrificed in order to ease some noble's path into the hereafter. He managed to persuade Ghezo to give the child to Queen Victoria to soften his refusal to leave the slave trade. "She would be a present from the King of the Blacks to the Queen of the Whites." (Forbes)

Little Aina is therefore uprooted again, this time being carted across an ocean to an entirely new culture. On the way she is baptised, acquires a new name — named for the Navy captain who rescued her, as well as the ship that brought her to England — and apparently learns English like a fish learns to swim. Now Sarah Forbes Bonetta, she is presented to Queen Victoria. Every account describes her as likeable, extremely talented and intelligent. Victoria is delighted by her wit and the ease with which she has stepped into the language and mores of her adopted country. Bonetta[1] is quickly established at court under the Queen's patronage but within a year she's acquired a lingering cough (attributed to the change in climate). At the age of eight, therefore, she is sent back across the Atlantic to Sierra Leone to be educated in a CMS[2] school in Freetown.

Four years later, in 1855, back across the Atlantic she comes again, this time to be fostered with a Reverend and Mrs Frederick Schön at Palm Cottage, Canterbury Road, Gillingham. Now, the Schöns had not long, themselves, returned from a stint in Sierra Leone. From there Frederick Schön, in 1841, had led an expedition up the Niger on behalf of the Church Missionary Society. He had been travelling with the then Mr Samuel Crowther who was to became the Right Rev Samuel Crowther, the Church of England's first BAME Bishop. The Crowthers and the Schöns remained friends and we can reasonably assume that the young Bonetta spends her adolescence being told stories of the expedition along the Niger.

Frederick Schön will have shared with Bonetta his conviction that the work in Africa was best done by indigenous converts. (This is a conviction established during his expedition as a result both of the extremely high body count among Europeans and of the favourable impression he saw created when the ex-slaves among his expedition read and expounded the Bible to the people along route.) Crowther went back and forth to Lagos, but it's likely he would have visited his friend when in England. Young Bonetta may have spent her evenings listening to the two men discuss missionary work. More importantly, Mrs Schön — and, likely, Mrs Crowther — would have told stories of their work in Sierra Leone.

---

[1] There is a pattern in writing in which men are referred to by their surnames, and women by their first names. Indeed this is often replicated when men and women introduce themselves, men usually including their surname and women generally introducing themselves on first name terms. Indeed, in western patrilineal traditions, women have generally not owned their surnames as they routinely signify the nearest male relative and are changed accordingly. Consistently referring to women by their surnames (where available), then, is a small token to go to reversing this.
[2] Church Mission Society

We know that women were excluded from the role of Missionary (capital 'm') because of the Victorian emphasis on preaching and professionalism, but they were nevertheless described as female missionaries (lowercase 'm'). They not only ran the schools and taught the women but were considered 'fellow labourers'. We have memoirs (usually posthumous) in which is recorded their collaboration with 'sister missionaries', which provides a network of public ministry of schooling, pastoral care, as well as a ministry of evangelism and catechesis which was so close to preaching as to lack only the name. The demand of the mission field was such that it required the labours of both sexes.

While such public ministry was not open to these women in their own country, returning missionaries were nevertheless expected to work hard advocating the cause. Certainly the missionary network was a tight one and dedicated to making more missionaries. The formal organisation of the missionary societies such as CMS was undergirded by a series of 'ladies networks,' committed to encouraging women to support the missionary endeavour. They encouraged women to set out to marry men chosen for their amenability to taking up the challenge of converting the 'heathen'. As Bonetta was reaching adulthood in the 1850s, women were even seeking recruitment in their own right. Mrs Shön, and very likely Mrs Crowther, will not have omitted encouraging the young women in their households to this task.

During this time Bonetta remains a celebrity in Victorian England as Queen Victoria's *exotic* goddaughter. At 19, for instance, she is invited to, and attends, the wedding of Queen Victoria's daughter Princess Alice. This is her 'other life', one of pageant and the 19th century equivalent of paparazzi. So it is perhaps not surprising that she is chosen to make a celebrity marriage. Her intended, James Pinson Labulo Davies, is a wealthy businessman, chosen — at least in part — to match her skin colour. He is also a philanthropist and missionary — part of the same network as the Schöns and Crowthers. He is a second generation Sierra Leonean: his parents had been rescued from slavery and brought to the British colony. Perhaps significantly in Bonetta's eyes, Davies is nearly twice her age and a widower.

The young émigré royal is not keen. As an inducement to change her mind she is is sent to live with a couple of elderly spinsters in Brighton in what Bonetta describes as a "desolate little pig sty." Given that she's used to being a regular visitor at the Royal Court, it seems unlikely that the place was terrible, but it appears to have been a clear signal of the life she could expect as a single woman without patronage. What to expect, in short, if she were to be disobliging. The young woman's resolve crumbles and the marriage receives Royal assent for August 1862 in Brighton. The wedding creates a media storm. The wedding party is made up of ten carriages with couples arranged in racial pairs, "White ladies with African gentlemen, and African ladies with White gentlemen." The story goes that there were so many people gathered round the church to see the celebrity couple that Bonetta herself had difficulty getting in.

After her marriage, Bonetta is returned once again to the African continent, this time to Lagos, where she begins to disappear from view. We know that she visits the Royal Court once more with her new baby, Victoria, who also becomes the Queen's goddaughter. Jesse Page in his 1892[3] account records, "she became most useful in the mission work at Lagos, and died full of joyful faith in her redeemer, in September 1880." The chronic cough which had plagued her since her first arrival in England has become tuberculosis. She is taken to Madeira to convalesce, to no avail. It seems typical of a life lived to other people's expectations that, although she specifically asks to be buried at sea, she is instead buried where she had died, in a place that has no connection to herself or her family.

Bonetta's story is symptomatic of a woman whose life is never really recorded apart from through the eyes of other people. All you see is glimpses of her at the edge of other people's priorities (although there is the exception of that one horrified reaction to her alternative future in Brighton). And yet, reading between the lines, we see a young woman who is repeatedly described as witty, intelligent, 'regal,' talented and cultured. She had survived early trauma and lived in three different royal courts at three very

---

[3] *The Black Bishop: Samuel Adjai Crowther*

different levels of status. As well as this, she had spent time in an English-style boarding school and a Kentish vicarage. If we include Madeira, she lived in six different countries and it's likely she learnt all the languages she came across. She died before she reached 40.

We can be confident that the 'useful work' that Bonetta engaged in Lagos would have been resourced by all her own talent and intelligence as well as the training she received from the Crowthers and the Schöns. Such an intelligent and resilient woman, surrounded by philanthropists (including the resources of her very rich husband), by the Church Mission Society and by the Church of England's first attempt at BAME leadership, how is she not going to be anything other than up to her elbows in the only work available to her? We only have Page's word, as to her personal conviction, but there are also traces of her gratitude to Captain Frederick Forbes. We know she was baptised. It is not unreasonable to suppose that she attributed some of her gratitude to the motivations of the man who rescued her from slavery. Certainly, there was a substantial and enthusiastic take-up among the people of Sierra Leone of the faith of their rescuers.[4] In any case, Sarah Forbes Bonetta, doyenne of Victoria's court, was not going to be content to sit at home as an *angel of the hearth.* Were it not for another woman more famous than she, we could describe her as Kent's most famous female missionary that you've never heard of.

But there is another woman whose proselytising endeavours are also regularly underestimated, whose weirdly sexualised statue[5] sits outside Canterbury's Diocesan Office.

---

[4] Although there is a telling line in Frederick Schön's journal, of one of his encounters along the Niger, in which his host says, '"Hitherto we thought it was so God's will, that the Black people should be slaves to the White people. White people told us we should sell slaves to them, and we sold them; and White people are now telling us not to sell slaves, and we will not sell them again:" and,' Frederick continues, 'as another justly added, "if White people give up buying, Black people will give up selling."'.

[5] Not only are her woollen garments strangely clingy, revealing curvature of boob, bum and thigh in a decidedly implausible fashion, but her derrière is most suspiciously shinier than the rest of her, as though more highly *polished*, for some reason.

It's predictable, if hardly commendable, that Bonetta isn't in our calendar of saints: neither is the Rt Rev Samuel Crowther despite his *documented* missionary zeal, his work translating the Bible into Yoruba, and his place as a Church of England first. I'll leave the reader to take a punt as to why this might be. **Bertha**, however, is a pivotal figure in the story of the Church in this country (and literally Anglo-Saxon) and she, too, is left by the wayside.

The reason for this, I suspect, is a minimising of the significance of mission-by-marriage which was a key method of the Frankish/Anglo-Saxon Church. Time and again across the Anglo-Saxon world we see political alliances sealed by marriages to Christian princesses, the terms of which are not only that she should keep her religion, but that she brought with her significant ecclesiastical backup. Time and again these marriages trigger the conversion of the Royal Court and then the kingdom. Time and again the credit goes to the accompanying clergy, rather than the women spearheading the mission.

Bertha, then, is usually treated as a codicil, a parenthesis. Augustine arrives (Bertha might get a nod of recognition for his invite) and apparently does all the work. The Church historian, the Venerable Bede, mentions that Ethelbert has heard of Christianity through Bertha, but even this seems like a very odd thing to say. Let me explain with a little background.

King Clovis of the Franks (who had married a Christian) was baptised in 496 A.D., a hundred years before his neighbour Ethelbert, and Christianity had had a noticeable presence in the north of what is now France for a good hundred years before that. Despite this, the south of England remained resolutely pagan. We don't know why. Certainly it wasn't cut off from its Frankish neighbour. We know there was a high level of social and economic interaction between the two regions. The sixth century King of Kent, Ethelbert, was the son of a man with a distinctly Frankish name (viz. Eormenric) and there is plenty of evidence in grave goods of a lively trade between Kent and its Frankish neighbour. It's simply not feasible that the people of Kent and Frankia were marrying each other and trading with each other but had not heard of one another's gods. Christianity was definately present in Britain, if not the dominant culture. For certain, then, Ethelbert was familiar with Christianity, Bertha or no Bertha.

It comes as a bit of a surprise, therefore, when Bede writes that the "fame of the Christian religion" reached Ethelbert through Bertha.[6] Bertha must have done more than simply introduce him to the concept. It looks more likely that she had to unpick some sort of deep seated Kentish prejudice against the religion.

Bertha is the daughter of Charibert, a distinctly unsavoury Frankish king who left Bertha's mother, Inoberga, because she objected to him sleeping with her servants. Charibert then slept with one sister and afterwards married the other (causing him to be excommunicated on the grounds of consanguinity). He had a child by a fourth woman (which didn't survive) and then married for a third time, being readmitted to the faith. I'm guessing he didn't have a lot of time for his daughter. However, someone educated her, and well. Her marriage to Ethelbert, c.580AD, coming with the usual clause of continuing-to-practice-her-religion with the clerical-support-group add-on, came to Pope Gregory's attention. (This is Gregory a.k.a. the Great, by the way, he who described the Anglo-Saxon slaves as 'angels,' being both beyond all reason surprised they hadn't heard of Christianity and excessively fond of bad puns.)

It is likely that Gregory sends Augustine into Kent because Ethelbert's influence over the south-east of England is considerable, but the presence of an intelligent, well read, reputable Queen — as Gregory describes her to be — we can only assume is also a factor. When Gregory writes to Bertha in 601 A.D. (very likely the year Ethelbert is baptised, but it seems the news hadn't yet reached Gregory), he tells Bertha that her reputation has spread as far as Constantinople. Certainly, when he writes to her, he expects her to have made more of an impact on her husband than, at the time of writing, he reckons she's had. (Which must have been galling for her, reading a letter rebuking her for not achieving the thing that

---

[6] It's a little bit like saying King Richard *discovered* Islam when he met Saladin, or Frodo Baggins *became aware of* elves when he met Legolas.

she has achieved.) Augustine, we are told, is quite impressed by her ("your Glory has exhibited itself towards our most reverend brother and fellow bishop Augustine"). It's a testament to his desire to work with her that Augustine's Cathedral is built so as to draw a line across the city between his cathedral and the church where Bertha worships. Her religion is by no means irrelevant to Augustine's campaign. Gregory is firmly of the opinion that it shouldn't be difficult for her to persuade her husband of the merits of Christianity *despite the fact that Kent has resisted Christianity for over a century*. It's pretty clear that Augustine is expected to do the heavy lifting in the field, but in the Royal Court, Gregory is waiting for Bertha to produce the goods.

And she does.

With Ethelbert's conversion we see significant numbers of other baptisms as well as considerable resources — including three cathedrals — being given to Augustine's mission. We also see the next cycle of mission-by-marriage. In about 625 A.D. Bertha's daughter, **Ethelburh**[7] is married to King Edwin of Northumbria. Again it is the complete package of continuing-to-practice-her-religion with the clerical-support add-on and again it bears fruit. Unfortunately, Edwin dies in battle not long after his baptism and Ethelburh returns to Kent where, we are told, with her brother's assistance, she founds a minster in Lyminge in about 633AD — probably the first women's house in the Augustinian movement (I'll come back to this). This Kentish princess is not half hearted, nor passive, in her application of her faith. Bede tells us that when Aidan shows up in Northumbria approximately five years later there was still a Christian community keeping the faith, despite Paulinus (Ethelberh's clerical support package) high tailing it back to Kent. Ethelburh's brief stint in Northumbria has had a lasting effect.

One of the attractions of the Royal marriage as a mission strategy is that it displays for the receiving court one of the significant advantages of mediaeval

---

[7] Æthelburh of Kent sometimes spelled Æthelburg, Ethelburga, Æthelburga, also known as Tate or Tata. See what joy there is to be had tracing the Kentish Royal family!

European Christianity: tech support.[8] The new Queen arrives literate and with a network that stretches across Europe, via her clerical companions, through the clergy ecclesiastical network. She is corresponding with European powers, including the Pope in Rome, and she brings clerks who are record keepers, lawyers, bookkeepers and historians. Increasingly, well-born Anglo-Saxon women are educated in the religious houses on the continent, with other wellborn European women, giving them a further political/ecclesiastical network which she can place at her husband's disposal. She brings more than pillow talk, she brings a whole civilisation with her.

At the heart of this civilisation lay the minster/abbey.

When the Romans left Britain in the early fifth century, Roman society did not really survive. The exercise of the next couple of hundred years was to build a whole new civilisation. The network of minsters built up by Kentish women, such as the one Ethelberh founded, was a series of linchpins to this new civilisation. Lyminge and the other houses that soon sprang up in Kent — Folkestone, Minster in Thanet, Minster in Sheppey *et cetera* — were the first stone buildings in their area. Lyminge was built at an important crossroads connecting the south coast with Canterbury; Folkestone and Minster-in-Thanet ditto, at ports connecting the Kentish kingdom with those of the Continent. Thanet, Sheppey, Hoo, Eastry: all these were ports and centres of communication. The excavation at Lyminge shows a significant settlement with evidence of industry and international trade.

The women in these houses were literate, corresponding with other religious houses, with popes and other ecclesiastical leaders, they were involved in church councils, and had an equitable share of patronage and influence. Their names are found on charters, wills, councils, financial settlements. These houses were hubs of significant economic and spiritual influence: the engines for the early Christian mission in Kent.

Which is not to say that they were in any way homogenous. The rule of St Benedict came slowly and

---

[8] My thanks to Ben Aaronovitch's *False Value* for this insight.

piecemeal into the women's houses of Kent, spliced, to different degrees, with the rules of Columbine and Cesarius. Nonetheless, at the heart of each minster was the singing[9] of the office,[10] and from this worship flowed the arterial blood of Christian education and service. The women read the Scriptures and committed them to memory, and were also busy copying, binding and illuminating manuscripts of the Bible, collections of liturgies, hagiographies and so forth. On top of this they were expected to take part in the running of the community: hospitality, housework, farmwork. Farmwork included caring for the oxen and sheep, whose wool they would card, spin, weave and then embroider the linen they had made. There would invariably be a small hospital, and a school attached to the minster where boys and girls were taught the faith with reading, writing, chanting, Latin grammar, illustrating, and the girls were also taught spinning, weaving, sewing and embroidery.

These Kentish minsters established themselves as missionary and catechistic endeavours, which provided pastoral and educational resources for the community. The women living in them were teachers, preachers, ministers of baptism, pastors, nurses. We know that they did not only attract women; men came to take their part in these houses both as avowed religious and as labourers, stewards, and muscle. These were not places where women went to 'flee the world.' The long list of Kentish women who were the celebrities of these houses — Ethelburh, Eanswythe, Saexburh, Eadburh, Domna Eafe, Mildthryth, Mildburh — they were not placid shrinking violets, hiding from the world in pious retreat. They were innovators, scholars and missionaries, invested in their communities and loved for centuries.

Much of their life is hidden by both time and language. Old English is not as interested in distinguishing between male and female, between fully fledged nun, novice and associate. They also had three different

---

[9] (so much so that when Hildegard's community in Bingen near the Rhine was placed under interdict in the 11th century, she complained more about the prohibition of singing than the loss of the sacraments!)
[10] A set of services of readings and prayers designed to reflect the rhythm of the day.

words for virgin[11], only one of which meant 'never had sex'. This means that it's not clear what happened when these houses began to fade out, as a country harried by Danish incursions could no longer afford to protect communities of women. The minsters that were once in key positions for trade and industry became the frontline of invasion by sea.

The minster model was essentially a peacetime endeavour. They required a certain complacency about how many children were needed, about the deployment of men-at-arms and the use of strategic land. They never flourished in war-torn regions — hence the fact that all of the minsters in Kent, bar one (and that one a Mercian endeavour) are in the east, far away from the border skirmishes with Mercia[12]. When war reached East Kent, the game changed. The royal and aristocratic houses previously content to provide an alternative occupation for women who were not romantically or maternally inclined, now needed the land, the soldiers and a strong line of heirs (and spares). The minsters closed, or became male only houses, and women's religious life faded from the history books.

Faded, but didn't disappear. It becomes nebulous, smoke-like, appearing in passing comments in a will, or an adjective in a charter. These women were never as interesting to historians, even at the time.[13] For starters they were the wrong sex and generally had less money. Once the organisation of women's religion no longer followed the same structures as the male establishments, the clerks and social commentators ceased to pay attention altogether. For much the same reasons (male) historians through the ages didn't think to look for them (not until recently) nor pay attention to the scant information in plain view. But we know the women were still there, still providing spiritual support, even if formal teaching was now off the agenda. There were women who were described as 'veiled', a 'vowess', or 'virgin' (with all the latter's

---

[11] *castitas*, stopped having sex; *iugalitas*, only having sex for procreation; *uirginitas*, never had sex.
[12] Basically the Midlands, but during the hay day of the Minster it came all the way down to London.
[13] The Venerable Bede doesn't seem to have heard of the houses at Folkestone or Sheppey, despite their regional significance, and seems to think that the English women-led minsters didn't run schools.

ambiguity). They were women who *owned* priests, who had maidservants sufficiently educated to recite the Psalter, women who bequeathed habits and office books, women who lived at arms-length from their families, cloistered but accessible. There were plenty of religious women, they just weren't attracting much attention.

So you see, the visibility of women's religion in Kent — as in the rest of the country — has come and gone in waves. Bertha began the first. We are now in what might be described as a third age of women's public mission in Kent, the second being in the high Middle Ages and the third started with the likes of Sarah Forbes Bonetta. In the in-between times, women are not silent or passive, though they are constrained. The mission becomes more domestic, closer to home, more fluid and adaptable. What the first and third ages have in common is a renewed awareness on the part of the Church of the pressing need for mission, of a world beyond itself. They have in common the need to harness the talents and energies of *all* available people "to do the work of an evangelist... proclaiming the glad tidings of salvation." ("Lydia", *Christian Ladies Magazine 6*, 1836)

Christianity is at heart a religion that faces the people not yet on board. The Church is at her best when she's a minority voice — Young David, rather than King David/Goliath. When she has less power, she is more humble. When her voice is quieter, she is more inclined to listen to the needs of the people she serves. When she's more focused on the task in hand, she is more likely to play nicely with the other children. When Christianity does not operate the hegemony, she has to use the full range of resources open to her. If necessity is the mother of invention, then invention's sister is opportunity. In times of necessity the ministry of women consistently becomes more prominent, more publicly exercised, harnessed under the yoke, not so much of their husbands, brothers, fathers, but of proclaiming the gospel.

Pioneers

When the dominant culture — the measure against which everyone is judged — is male, then the business of being a female Christian is always to some extent an exercise in discovering how to translate a masculine pattern into a feminine form. In any society, women's lives have different rhythms, and usually a different sphere and different priorities. At its most basic level, this translation exercise could simply mean working out how to dress — for example when women in the 20th century were ordained deacon then priest, or a century before, when Isabella Gilmore was trying to decide what the deaconess should wear. On occasion this has meant trying to fit the same vocation into a much smaller societal role — or else pushing back against societal stereotypes and expectations to make space for vocation. When women preached, for instance, sometimes they created their own context in which to do it, like the Anglo-Saxon abbesses, sometimes they didn't call it preaching, like the Victorian missionaries, and sometimes women simply said, "listen to me," and preached, like the radical protestants of the 17th century.

Just occasionally this feminising of male patterns involves creating new territory, new roles and new identities with which to equip women in the Church. This chapter concerns the innovators, the church women who have made new spaces or shapes of ministry so that they and other women can answer the call of God: the Pioneers.

In the previous chapter, I explored the missionary dimension to the Anglo-Saxon Minster. One of the reasons the minsters were as effective as they were was because of the abbesses that ran them. In the heady whirl of creating a new Christian society almost from scratch, these women forged an ecclesiastical role of communal and sacramental significance only, possibly, matched by the female parish priests of today — or possibly not even until we had bishops. Take **Eadburh**.

Before we do, however, a word of explanation, because to talk about Eadburh, we also need to discuss Ethelburh — to whom you were introduced in Chapter 1 — and possibly another Eadburh, because, depending on how you count, she's up to three different women. In fairness, it was a common name, and the whole name business seems to have been taken a lot less seriously in those days — more of an art than a science.[1]

The 11th century chronicler, Goscelin, writes of Ethelburh that she is buried at Lyminge, and goes on, "*sed uulgo ibi nominabator quaedom sancta Eadburga.*" Herein lies a bucket of confusion, because this little phrase can be translated either, "but a certain St Eadburh was commonly named there," or, "but she was commonly named there as a certain St Eadburh." These are two very different statements[2], but as the cult of St Eadburh grows, the latter interpretation dominated. Watch carefully, because what we end up with is a woman who is at one and the same time the daughter of Queen Bertha (who d. c.610AD) and the successor of the Abbess Mildthryth[3] (d. c.730AD). This is tricky, because Mildthryth is Bertha's great great granddaughter, which would make Eadburh/Ethelburh a woman who is both Mildthryth's great great aunt and also someone who lived long enough to bury that same Mildthryth. Not itself *impossible*, but given Mildthryth herself seems to have had a long and fruitful life, unlikely.

The cult of Eadburh is thus a conflation of (A) Bertha's (widowed) daughter, Ethelburh, who we know married Edwin and then, on being widowed, returned to Kent, and who may have founded Lyminge; (B) Mildthryth's successor, Eadburh, who we know was abbess of Minster-in-Thanet; and (C) (virginal) Eadburh who had a corpse and cult at Lyminge. Admittedly, the two Eadburhs (women B & C) are plausibly the same person, but as Goscelin is quick to point out, the

---

[1] In the following attempt to disentangle something that looks like a biography, I am greatly indebted to Rosalind Love's article on Eadburh for the Société des Bollandistes.
[2] "*she was with Eadburh*," or "*she was called Eadburh.*"
[3] I will tell you Mildthryth's story ... eventually.

chances of her also being Ethelberh (woman A) are vanishingly small. The advantage of this conflation of all three to the cult of St Eadburh (which by the 10th century had been absorbed into the community of St Gregory's in Canterbury) is that they were able to add to their saintly relics both the aristocratic credibility of Ethelberh (A) and the virginal credibility of Eadburh (C) *and* an association with the awesomeness of Mildthryth (Eadburh B). (As far as St Gregory's is concerned, there is also a massive beef about the location of Mildthryth which is mixed in with this narrative, but we'll come to that later. One muddle at a time.)

The 10th century writers were interested in Eadburh on two fronts: (1) there was a general attempt to recruit the holy dead against the forces of chaos and darkness represented by the concerted (pagan) Viking attacks towards the end of the 10th century; and (2) there was also something of a rewriting of the nature of sanctity in women under the influence of the European Carolingian reforms.

(A quick word on the Carolingian reforms, because they'll keep coming up. The 10th and 11th century reforms responded to the desire for uniformity driven by Charlemagne in the 9th century, and the centralisation of power in England, which were expressed both organisationally and theologically. The push was for all religious communities to be organised the same, but also for a much more linear understanding of the sacraments. The sacraments were being more sharply defined and numbered — we're beginning to settle on seven — and much more focused on the ministry of priests. Social changes to the status of women meant that they were increasingly infantilised. They were also not trusted with men not related to them, and/as the double houses[4] were phased out. The Carolingian reforms on the continent were not *imposed* on the Church in this country but they did change the culture. They were the context of King Edgar's reforms that followed in England under Dunstan, Æthelwold and Oswald in the late 10th century. They give us a good idea of what women were doing, because the reforms were explicitly stopping it.)

---

[4] (Monasteries that were for both sexes)

Towards this object (2), then — the redefining of women — we have this strange splicing of royal pedigree (with all of the international connections that implies) with virginal purity (in the teeth of the royal saint in question being a widow), and the emphasis on her retreat from the world. Towards the former object (1) — Defence Against the Dark Arts — we have a wonderful array of post-mortem miracles attributed to Eadburh, two of which involved her making disrespectful men explode,[5] two concern her abilities to effect miracles over some considerable distance from Lyminge, and one her ability to protect her own interests. This is a saint, we are led to believe, who is more than capable of defending her own, given a little respect. It's not a comfortable mix with objective (2), but nobody seems to mind.

What makes her interesting to us — or at least to me — is the light shone by her story on the world of the early Anglo-Saxon abbess, because part of her story has become the story of Eadburh of Minster-in-Thanet (Eadburh B). Our 10th century biographer, while rooting her sanctity in virginal otherworldliness, as is proper to the new regime of women being cloistered and apart, describes a woman whose holiness is demonstrated in active ministry. She and Mildthryth, her predecessor, are not only committed to constant prayer, with the singing of psalms and liturgy, along with vigils, fasting and good works, but to rigorous ('manly') study, to the teaching of the women in their care and to *preaching*.

Furthermore, Eadburh takes a unilateral decision that Mildthryth is worth veneration and gathers the resources to build the new stone church in an age of wooden buildings. The tomb she builds is so substantial that in one version of the translation of Mildthryth to Canterbury, the monks endeavouring to steal her corpse make so much noise extracting her body that the extraction plan nearly fails. Then, when living so near the coast begins to look risky, Eadburh

---

[5] In the first case it is a Viking who dies through a "bloody purging of his bowels" after dragging a cowering priest off Eadburh's tomb. In the second it is a thief who, in the course of a conversation that takes place in the public toilet, swears his innocence on "God and St Eadburh whose place I can see now." The sainted Eadburh, presumably outraged at his perjury, causes him to void his guts out of his arse. So let that be a lesson to you. Perjury is really frowned upon in Lyminge.

relocates her community, joining the minster at Lyminge. She is the pastor of her community and its steward.

The abbesses of the first couple of centuries of Christianity in Kent drew from an Anglo-Saxon playbook in which women were expected to be cultically active.[6] These abbesses, however, took it further, liberated as they were by the missionary call and by the blank slate of the new Kentish Church. In the fluid context of the creation of a new civilisation, with a migrant population and a new religion, these well-connected and well-educated women forged a ministry to accompany the missionary powerhouses that were the women's minsters. Like a bishop, the abbess was consecrated, wore a pectoral cross and carried a pastoral staff. Like a priest, the rite of her making included being given a chalice, and she heard confessions and provided penance, blessed her community and conducted last rights. Like a deacon, she preached and interpreted Scripture, baptised and administered Holy Communion. The steward of her community, she negotiated property boundaries, water rights and organised the finances (and location!) of the community. She was second only to the Bishop — and only by a little bit. Eadburh's was a culture in which abbesses were ranked with queens[7].

This cult of Eadburh, reworked and retold as it is, shows that the memory of these women's ministry is still persistent in the light of the 'reforming' of women's religion that was taking place at the time. Even as the role of women was shrinking, these clerical abbesses were remembered as forces to be reckoned with. Even as the likes of Eadburh were being replaced with pale copies, Eadburh's story and relics were treasured as a reminder of what had been.

It was told to women who had become defined as meek, helpless, spiritually frail and at risk of running amok if not kept under the firm leadership of the Bishop. The abbesses had been stripped of their authority and their liturgical roles. The sisters of the community were no longer allowed so much as to

---

[6] Women were buried, often, with respect, with keys and with cultic items.
[7] Literally – there are lists in which the kings, bishops and abbots are under separate headings, but the queens and abbesses together.

touch the altar linen. The abbesses went from being an international network of highly educated — and usually wealthy — women, to being confined to the cloister, wholly dependent on visiting men for the sacraments, for financial viability and strength of arms. They were forbidden to leave the premises, even on pilgrimage, without the Bishop's say-so. What Goscelin witnessed, and tried to translate in an entirely new ecclesiastical context for women, was the echo of a past age.

Even then — even then — the role of the abbess, hamstrung though it was, had considerable clout, as we'll see when we come to the story of St Sepulchre's Abbey (chapter 6). This may be why, when the Rochester Diocese finally gets a significant religious house of its own, under Gundulf's diocesan reforms, he is so reluctant to appoint an abbess until Avicia practically pries the pastoral staff from his dying hands[8]. Despite their clear misogyny, the Carolingian reforms were not the end of women's innovation in their response to the call of God, by any means.

For most of the Middle Ages women remain, in Kent, in the places allotted to them — which isn't to say there weren't some interesting workarounds. As we saw in the previous chapter, women's religious life shrank to the domestic sphere or, as we'll see in chapter 5, was exercised vicariously. It was still vibrant and influential but it was discreet for a century or two. Even as women's religious houses began to gain traction again in the high Middle Ages, the ministry of women was still focused on the workaround rather than the radical.

Then, in the fervour of the Reformation, something changed. When ideas were once again in flux and society in turmoil, women again started to push against the lines that had been drawn for them. The Protestant emphasis on a personal, informed faith and on the priesthood of all believers encouraged women to think that their spirituality mattered and that their

---

[8] adamant that no monk is going to not tell her what to do ... er. No really, the record has it that she's quite assertive about *not* being told what to do. She "swore fidelity and subjection to the very same bishop, his successors, and the holy church of Rochester, because she would not be persuaded, either by him or by another person, to dissolve the aforesaid subjection." (Textus Roffensis, translation by Dr Chris Monk). I blame internalised Carolingian reforms.

encounter with Scripture — personal and informed as it was — had primacy over the injunctions of the Church. The teachings of the Reformers lead women to believe that their own religious agency was essential to the health of their soul. A new kind of church woman arose, who had something to say and was determined to say it.

First among them were the Lollards and their successors, the Anabaptists. The Lollards' meetings were often hosted by women, where the Bible and the prayers were read in English and learnt by heart. They were egalitarian and anticlerical. Joan Bocher — whose story we'll come to soon — was at the centre of the Lollard/Anabaptist community in Canterbury with links to the Reformers in London. In between running a house church, smuggling Bibles into London and repeatedly being arrested, she found the time to be married twice and to gain a reputation as a preacher. She was not the only one.

Across Kent, women decided that this new, individualist Christianity, with its personal responsibility, could not be left to their husbands and brothers alone. It was too important (and they clearly didn't think their men were doing it very well). The anonymous tract of 1641 records *A Discoverie of Six Women Preachers, in Middlesex, Kent, Cambridge, and Salisbury. With a Relation of their Names and Doctrine, Pleasant to be Read but Horrid to be Judged of. Their Names Are These: Anne Hempstall, Mary Bilbrow, Ioanne Bauford, Susan May, Elizab. Bancroft, Arabella Thomas*. It lists **Joanne Bauford** and **Susan May** as women in Kent (Faversham and Ashford respectively) who are not only preaching, but preaching radicalism.

> "*their onely reafon or caufe of preaching was, that there was a deficiency of good men, wherefore it was but fit, that virtuous women fhould fupply their places, they were (men they did mean) good for nothing ...*"

People came in droves to hear them, in their "corners" to applaud their "Sacerdocticall" [sic] function and to witness this thing that was happening in Kent. The women were very clear that they could no longer depend on men to define their faith for them, nor indeed were they obliged to remain loyal to men "which did not love Puritans," for such men were fathered by the Devil, apparently.

This tradition thrived among the Dissenters, being anticlerical and so having more room for women's ministry. The Quakers, in particular, gave women the right to speak during meetings from the get go (in the 1650s). Women were fairly swiftly given agency over their own affairs in the administration of the Quaker communities which led pretty quickly to women travelling alone on their own business and publishing their own writings. Equality became for the Quakers a watchword, a definitive quality of the Christian life. Elizabeth Fry, for example, was unexceptionally authorised as a minister in 1811.

These women remained in the minority, however, hearing a call to spiritual agency which, in most of the establishment, was not intended for them. The enthusiasm with which so many women took on board the pro-offered individualism and autonomy of Protestantism (who were described by the likes of Robert Parsons as "impudent," "presumptuous," and sexually immoral) was firmly shut down. Luther's antipathy to religious orders spread to the whole Reformed Church. With the dissolution of the monasteries, a significant harbour of religious independence as well as artistic and intellectual freedom was closed to women. Their education and even their conversation were limited. Marriage and family life were declared necessary for women to restrain their sexuality and focus their minds on salvation-by-childbirth. It was beginning to look as though the Reformation had made women less responsible for their own salvation, rather than more.

Many women exercised their ministry by proxy, marrying men who were either ordained or, as we saw with the women who wanted to be missionaries, malleable to the vocation of their espoused wife. However, the emphatic domesticity of women's religion meant that they were increasingly expected to tend to the poor and to be hospitable as an extension of their generally caring and supportive sphere. This meant that in the next round of social upheaval, under the industrial revolution, women were prime candidates to step into the gap in social care created by the massive overpopulation of the cities. Once again necessity proved the mother of emancipation.

As women stepped into the vacancy, two women in Kent were pioneers of forgotten ministries for the female sex: the deacon and the contemplative. Both of these two women — Isabella Gilmore and Harriet Stewart — were convicted by the importance of a woman's personal vocation (a shocking concept in a world in which women's identity was almost entirely subsumed into their husband's). In the mid-19th century, society was just about tolerating women's social action within the context of communities of women. Both Gilmore and Stewart had other ideas. Both pushed this new model into a more radical direction. Gilmore took women's vocation out of the religious houses of the deaconess movement as it was when she found it, and dragged it into the parish and towards ordained ministry. Stewart went in the opposite direction, taking the newly formed sisterhoods and turning them inwards and upwards, demanding that women's contemplative life be taken seriously.

Harriet Emily Stewart, being born in 1828, hit adulthood just as Priscilla Sellon (you can find her in the Church of England calendar of saints, under November) was setting up one of the first Anglican communities of vowesses in Devonport. The movement to reinvent the religious life within Anglicanism was the result of a heady mix of Romanticism and Tractarianism. Shelley and Wordsworth were painting dreamy pictures of monastic ruins and haunted landscapes, while men like Edward Pusey and John Mason Neale were calling for a second Reformation to bring the Church of England back to her primitive roots.

The romanticism of the poets fed into the Church's reaction against the unsettling effects of the Enlightenment and the scientific revolution, causing her to bury herself in mysticism, hagiography and emotive simplicity. Meanwhile, the Oxford Movement pushed back against perceived secularising impetus of the state, and the liberalising impetus in the Church, by emphasising the Church's historic roots and connections. The perceived weakening of social structures encouraged nostalgia on all sides. In consequence, the Victorian Church in England was gripped by a renewed sense of vocation and the sacredness of time. The resuscitation of the sisterhoods was, however, most significantly assisted by the gaping social need created by the industrial revolution.

Between 1780 and 1860 there was an unprecedented migration from villages to the cities — by 1850 c.40% of the population of London had migrated in from the countryside or from Ireland and the European continent. Then, in the second half of the 19th century the population of England and Wales more than doubled, from nearly 16 million in 1841, to over 32.5 million in 1901. The infrastructure of the cities was completely unable to cope. Ecclesial, civic, legal, educational: all of these were inadequate, and the health and sanitation of the cities collapsed.

> *"In district of East London they lived, family to a room, in wooden sheds or closed courts or tenements, without privies and sometimes with an open sewer running down the centre of the street and likely to overflow in wet weather; the houses dirty beyond description, potato peel or gristle or bones thrown into corners. At Bethnal Green a row of pig sties emptied their refuse into a neighbouring pool of stagnant water, and in some streets lay pools polluted with dead cats and dogs and rubbish."* (Chadwick, *The Victorian Church*, part one)

Roman Catholic nuns were already moving among the slums of those urban corners sheltering French and Irish immigrants, and the Puseyites were determined to put English gentlewomen alongside them. Caught in this pastoral fervour, then, young Stewart joins the new Sisterhood of Mercy working among the poor of Devonport. In 1863 she moves to the Society of St Margaret, East Grinstead, where she becomes a novice before returning to Devonport with a new name, Hilda, and increased fervour.

Meanwhile Joseph Lyne, "for whom the epithets eccentric and erratic seem insufficient,"[9] an Anglican distinctive deacon, establishes the first English enclosed order in 300 years. Originally for men, the community acquired an associated women's community. Lyne seemed to have a talent for alienating people, and the two communities struggle to find a stable location, but eventually the women's house — the Community of SS Mary and Scholastica — settled in an old farmhouse at Feltham in Middlesex. It is at this point that Mother Lydia at Devonport suggests Stewart for prioress of the new community.

Stewart clearly arrives with the bit between her teeth. From this point she calls herself Mother Hilda OSB (Order of St Benedict), the first Church of England woman to take the epithet, although it's not entirely clear with what authority she does so. She also takes to wearing a pectoral cross. Her arrival seems to trigger a rebellion among the nuns against Lyne's "eccentricities". In 1878, shortly after Hilda's arrival, all but three of the nuns secede and Lyne is evicted. Not taking this quietly, Lyne excommunicates them, complete with black vestments and tolling bell. Undaunted, the Community of SS Mary and Scholastica, under Hilda's leadership, retains the farmhouse. The remains of Lyne's double house slowly folds under its financial demands and the weight of his "eccentricity".

Still, the viability of Mother Hilda's community isn't looking good, either. The small community of contemplatives is struggling in a Church suspicious of nuns in general, and enclosed nuns in particular. The active sisterhoods were just about tolerated on the grounds that they were engaged in women's work, attending to the great sea of poor and distressed humanity that was urban Victoriana. These nuns of Hilda's were looking suspiciously papist and un-English. It was pivotal, then, that not long after the sisters seceded — about 1883 — the community encounters Charlotte Boyd (of whom more, anon).

---

[9] A measure of this so-called eccentricity is that the self-styled "Father Ignatius Llanthony" described himself as "the divinely appointed and inspired apostle of Jesus Christ as well as the man chosen by God to restore the cloistered life for men and women in the Church of England," which probably tells you all you need to know.

Although the two women don't seem to hit it off, Boyd becomes an associate and a patron to the sisters. By the end of the decade, the community is semi-peripatetic again. They lose the farmhouse, and their next home in Twickenham, to discover that Boyd has bought the house at Malling Abbey, the site of a mediaeval monastic community. Hilda is hopeful that her little community can move in.

Do you remember that I said Boyd and Hilda didn't hit it off? Well, Boyd wasn't altogether keen on Hilda as a tenant. She offered Malling Abbey to three other communities first, but none of the others were prepared to saddle themselves with the significant costs of running the place, let alone the work of restoration. Even Hilda is daunted. "Our going to Malling required very great trust in God's divine providence." Nevertheless, she sets about raising the money and on 12 April, 1893, the Community of SS Mary and Scholastica moves in. They travel down from Twickenham in two parties, in train and in horse and cart, stopping on the way to say sext and vespers. Arriving after dark, the community is met by Boyd at the old Pilgrim Gate. Boyd has lined the path for them with candles and they process in chanting the 68th Psalm[10].

The place is a wreck. On the first night, the sisters sleep on the floor. The old church has been turned, during its domestic usage, into a scullery and a milk shed. The earthen floor is exposed and there is no roof. Hilda arranges for boards to be laid down in the old charterhouse, and converts it to the chapel.

A local cleric describes the chapel some little while later, and this description vividly impresses the mystic Teilhard de Chardin to fire a shot across the active-or-nothing bow of the sisterhoods ship.

> "The contemplative sensitised and animated all things because she believed; and her faith was operative because her very pure soul placed her

---

[10] "...Sing to God, sing praises to his name; lift up a song to him who rides upon the clouds—his name is the Lord— be exultant before him.

Father of orphans and protector of widows is God in his holy habitation.

God gives the desolate a home to live in; he leads out the prisoners to prosperity..." (Psalm 68.4-6)

> *near to God. ... And yet, if we could see the 'light invisible' as we can see clouds or lightning or the rays of the sun, a pure soul would seem as active in this world, by virtue of its sheer purity, as the snowy summits whose impassable peaks breathe in continually for us the roving powers of the high atmosphere."*
> *(*The Divine Milieu)

Here the country's first enclosed community laid its roots for a time, and secured the peace with which visitors are familiar. The community not only flourished in its own right, but was a resource for other communities, seeding a new house for men, for example, via their chaplain Arthur Dale.

Hilda struggles with her health and in the last years of her primacy the community loses a degree of its vim. By the time she dies in 1906 she has lost some of her reputation for leadership and determination. Still, when the reins are passed on, the foundations are such that her successor flourishes, inheriting a significantly restored infrastructure and gaining new postulants, so that she is able to extend the mediaeval guesthouse which is still the core of the Abbey's outreach today. By 1906, many of the people with whom Hilda shared her vocation have submitted to Rome. Indeed, soon after she dies, her community does convert[11]. Nevertheless, Hilda dies as she lived: the first self-styled Benedictine abbess in the Reformed Church of England.

Moreover, she has taken the window of opportunity created for her by the expansion of women's ministry into the slums of the urban centres, and turned it into something quite different. England was full of women stepping into the manifest breach, but for Hilda the priority was prayer. For 300 years the acceptable role of women had been entirely domestic and practical. Hilda re-forged an identity and mission that was focused on the eternal, and its impact is still tangible in the Diocese of Rochester to this day.

---

[11] Mthr Scholastica decamps before submitting to Rome, on the grounds that the community has outgrown the site, but her inquiries about the Canterbury clause in the Trust strongly suggest the transition has been on her mind for a while.

Isabella Gilmore branches off from the same beaten track in almost entirely the opposite direction. Born within a year of Sarah Forbes Bonetta, in 1842, Gilmore is still a little girl when Hilda (still Harriet Stewart) joins the Devonport sisters. By the time Hilda is just meeting Charlotte Boyd for the first time, Gilmore is newly widowed and looking for something to fill the loss of a much loved husband. The general Victorian expectation is for her to divert her energies to her extended family, and indeed, on the sudden death of her brother Rendell in 1884 Gilmore does take on responsibility for his eight children (aged, at the time, two and above). By then, however, Gilmore has decided that needlepoint and Companionship are not her bag. Scandalously, despite not needing the money, she gets a job. She trains as a nurse at Guy's Hospital on the back of Florence Nightingale's reforms. It is hard to express how radical this is. Respectable married women did not go about unescorted by a maid/parent/husband and most emphatically did not take lodgings away from her family. Her mother is so scandalised that the two are alienated from each other until Gilmore's mother is close to death, decades later. *"Women today will hardly realise what it was then for a lady to work & I had many troublious [sic] times to go through with my relations, many hard unkind things were said,"* writes Gilmore, later, in an extravagance of understatement. This separation is painful to Gilmore for the rest of her adult life. At her ordination, only her brother-in-law John Gilmore, and her sister and brother, Emma and William Morris (yes, *that* William Morris) are present from her family.

Taking on eight children puts a slight dent on her ambition, but is not enough to keep Gilmore tethered to home and hearth. Instead she starts to look for some voluntary occupation just at the point where Bishop Thorold of Rochester is looking for a solution to the problem of ministering to the slums of his newly reorganised diocese.

In 1877 the dioceses of London, Winchester and Rochester had been reorganised to create the Diocese of St Albans. Before then, most of Rochester Diocese had been in rural Essex. Thorold describes the new diocese into which he is consecrated as a Cinderella diocese of the poorer bits of London rejected by London and Winchester.

> *"All were displeased with the new diocese, which people said had only by accident or afterthought been allowed to include even those few prosperous suburbs now allocated to it."* ('The life and work of Bishop Thorold', CH Simkinson)

Thorold, who up till now had ministered in North London, was deeply shocked by the living conditions of the people in his diocese and vividly aware of his clergy's inability to cope.

Plan-the-first had been to deploy the new Salvation Army, but he had found them a tad excitable. His next solution had been to try and set up a Lay Helpers' Association, but there had been little enthusiasm for the role to be found. (Plan 2b, seems to have been the setting up of a sisterhood — perhaps even Mtr Hilda's community which moved into Malling Abbey two years after Thorold's translation to Winchester.) Plan the third involved the new network of Deaconess Houses that were spreading out from London, but Thorold wanted somebody to rework the idea first.

The version that had been brought across from Germany by Elizabeth Ferard (we'll revisit this in chapter 8) was in many ways the Protestant-ising of the religious houses springing up in the Anglo-Catholic wing of the Church. It was a solution to the unease felt by the general population at the autonomy and 'Papism' of the sisterhoods, that aimed to retain women's passion and labour in the service of the poor. So while Ferard's deaconess movement still organised themselves in houses, they were not in convents, and the deaconesses were expected to offer lifelong service, but there were no life vows. They were under the supervision of a head deacon, but made no vows of obedience to a mother superior; they were expected to remain single, but they were not 'celibate'. Duck, walk, quack, etc. but it was important to the Deaconess movement to avoid the language of the *Roman Catholic* religious life. Most importantly, Ferard constantly emphasised the authority of the Bishop over the deaconess houses so, fear not, gentlemen, a man was still in charge. The authority of the mother abbess had emphatically not been recreated.

It takes a while for Thorold to get Gilmore on board (eight children is one hell of a responsibility to juggle with, while creating a whole new order of ministry). At length he passes to her his determined vision of bringing love to the darkest corners of his diocese, where poverty, as he says, is not just in terms of money but of air, light, space and water. Once she takes on the project, not being a woman of half-measures, Gilmore is very clear that her deaconess order is not a variation of the religious vocation but rather of the vocation to ordained ministry.

Gilmore looks at the service to which society was calling women, the 'women's work' of tending the sick, caring for the vulnerable, for children, for orphans, working in hospitals, prisons, asylums, teaching children, and concludes that these were the marks of the ministry of a deacon. In her booklet, "The Deaconess and her Ministry," Gilmore emphasises the New Testament and the Early Church precedent for her assertion that the deaconess is essentially the same order as the deacon. It is, she argues, a personal vocation to service, confirmed by the Church in the person of the Bishop. Under her influence Thorold ordains deaconesses with the laying on of hands and issues them letters of orders — features which, since the Carolingian reforms, had until then been reserved entirely for the ordination of male priests and deacons.

The key thing, for Gilmore, was that her deaconesses were based not in the deaconess house, but in the parish, licensed to the parish and to the incumbent. She flips the Ferard model. For Ferard, the principal loyalty of the deaconess is to the deaconess order and to her training house, and only secondarily to the incumbent and his parish. Gilmore's deacons, on the other hand, are released from the house to work in the parish alongside the parish clergy, so that she *"is licensed to the parish, receives her own stipend, and is entirely independent of the Head Deaconess, but she is responsible to her Vicar and her Bishop."* (Gilmore, annual report, 1896). Gilmore is convinced this is the primitive (ie Early Church) model.

Experience has also shown her that allegiance to a structure separate from the parish undermines loyalty and responsiveness both on the part of the deaconess and on the part of the parish clergy. For Gilmore, the deaconess house is there for support, not oversight.

Like the other Victorians we'll look at, Gilmore is still a creature of her time, for all her innovation. She believes in the 'natural authority' that the middle classes have over the poor. She sees the deaconess not only theologically but culturally as the counterpart to the English clergyman. This does not mean that she keeps herself apart, though. She is genuinely shocked by the living standards of the slum tenements; she is adamant that her deaconesses should roll up their sleeves and muck in. Whereas Ferard's deaconesses avoid "everything vulgar and indelicate," Gilmore's are expected to be confident in London slums and enter the grimmest accommodation without flinching. They are to fill the gaps in a parish system overwhelmed by urbanisation, which often meant working across any boundaries that obstructed the endeavour: unlike William Booth[12], Gilmore works with any organisation in the field. "The more we know about each other's work," she says, "the more we help each other, and can send the right people to the right places." She is not precious.

Two stories, I think, exemplify Gilmore's commitment and ministry. The first is that on the eve of Gilmore's own ordination she puts all her rings, including her wedding ring, aside as a gesture of her wholehearted commitment to her new ministry. Giving them up is not a light gesture. "It was not vanity, but all that they had meant to me." She has them melted down and added to a chalice that she has made for the chapel at Gilmore House. Thereafter, like the clergyman perpetually in holy black, Gilmore is seen only in deaconess blue.

The other is of her response to the discovery that few in the patch in which she serves are baptised. On investigation[13] she hears it is in part because the women in the slums rarely leave their own house and

---

[12] Of that other great endeavour to address the same problem, namely the Salvation Army.
[13] Gilmore has the radical practice of talking to the people whom she wishes to serve.

even more rarely leave the small selection of streets that is their community. Should they muster the audacity to do so, Gilmore found, they still will not go to church on a Sunday because they cannot dress for church, having only one set of ragged clothes. Gilmore browbeats her incumbent into offering a baptism on a weekday evening. The sceptical cleric gives her a service slot of half an hour, just before the parish meeting. The service overruns by a full hour and 93 children are baptised. Case irrefutably made, these 'public baptisms' become a regular feature in the parish and are run with near military organisation by Gilmore.

Gilmore's deaconesses changed the structure of ministry in the Church of England. Between 1860 and 1919 431 deaconesses are ordained, 76 of whom — over a fifth — for the Rochester Diocese. True, there remains during her lifetime significant resistance to Gilmore's vision of an order of deaconesses that is on a par with their male equivalent. This means that the lack of hierarchical structure and proper definition of the role hamstrings the order. At length the numbers fall, despite the need for their ministry. A significant chunk of the objection lies in admitting women to Holy Orders, with the authority and independence of vocation that gives to them. The rest is mixed up in the Protestant opposition to celibacy, on account of the association with religious orders through Ferard, and in Gilmore's subversion of traditional domestic gender roles. Still, throughout her life, even after her retirement from her role as the head deaconess of the Rochester Diocese, Gilmore pushes hard for acknowledgement of her deaconesses' authority under Christ and for the significance of a woman's personal vocation. There is no doubting that she laid the foundations for the ordination of women to the diaconate in 1987, and to the priesthood in 1994.

All of her writings are full of her love of God and her love of the people that she served. She retires in 1906 and dies in 1923. By 1936 she is largely forgotten.

Gilmore, Stewart, Joan Bauford, Susan May and Eadburh all forged a ministry within the Church for the Church. All these women had clear vocations to the service of God within the Church, having a desire to serve which stretched well beyond the tidy confines of kith and kin. Theirs was a desire not simply to the 'women's work' of tending to the sick and the marginalised, but the vision of working within the structures and systems of the Church — even if the pattern that they used had been dormant for centuries or even more than a millennium. They were innovators, and servants of the Church (regardless of the level of that same Church's enthusiasm for their service). They were essentially ecclesiastical, and utterly determined.

Reformers and rebels

The wider Church may have been a little uneasy with the ecclesiastical innovators of the previous chapter; she left the women of this chapter dead, homeless and unemployed (not necessarily in that order). These women, instead of trying to work within the system, fought it. They took on King/Queen and country for the sake of the vision that God had given them. You may not agree with them — Bocher, in particular, still falls outside what most people consider orthodox theology — but theirs was a struggle for freedom of religion. They stood their ground because they believed that truth was more important than their own safety. They spoke up because they thought they had something to say that made a difference to people's ability to encounter the divine. It may not have ended well for them, but the hagiographer John Foxe is emphatic that their witness and example strengthens others — and other women in particular.

For one turbulent period in European history, the Church's enthusiasm was the death of a number of women (and men) in Kent. In the 16th century in particular, not only was there a widespread spirit of religious radicalism and rebellion, but the prevailing wind kept changing course. Women who were orthodox in the one decade found themselves to be heretics in another. Thus, Anne Askew died in 1546 for believing that Holy Communion is "a peece of bread"; by the time Joan Bocher dies in 1550, this is the official doctrine of the Church of England. Several women in Mary's reign are executed for keeping the faith taught to them in the previous reign. One of the curious elements of the era, however, was that a remarkable number of women refused to keep their head down and obey their husband/Church, choosing instead the dangerous line of ferocious personal integrity.

This was one of the conundrums for those Protestants describing the women of the period. Social convention expected women to be silent and obedient, modest and passive; the women of Foxe's *Book of Martyrs* were outspoken, abrasive, learned and assertive bordering on cocky. Convention had it that women were weak and inconsistent, but the 16th century martyrs stood up to cruelty and abuse which was often drawn out over months. With the closing of the convents, the only remaining role for women was in domestic obedience and service, yet many of these women defied and abandoned their husbands. While some of them refused to flee for the sake of their children, others refused to recant, despite leaving dependent children and even infants behind them. Only four of Foxe's 50-odd female martyrs die with their husbands.

Thus Robert Parsons, a Jesuit and less than impartial commentator on Foxe's sixteenth century compilation of martyrs, takes a very dim view of these women and of their hagiographer. He was scornful of John Foxe for recounting their 'shameful' history and, as Parsons reckons, embellishing them. (He basically wrote that no woman could be as articulate as the women Foxe described.) Parsons, like many of the women's accusers at the time, assumed that if they were so out of control as to try and define their own spirituality, they must also have been sexually immoral.

Conversely, Foxe revelled in the paradox. Where Parsons saw disorderly women refusing the proper order of things, Foxe saw the power and spirit of God shining through women's, as he saw it, inherent weakness. He is adamant of their simplicity and purity. His "seely, poore women" were often depicted in terms of clay jars revealing most powerfully the golden treasure. Only God, he argued, could inspire such faithfulness and zeal. Foxe was adamant that these weak women revealed God's strength, these uneducated women proclaimed God's wisdom and the speech of those who ought not to be heard in public revealed the Word of God. As Foxe had it, "God geueth strength many times, when most weakness is."

Take **Margery Polley**, for example, the first woman to die in Mary's reign. Foxe tells us she is a widow who had hardly ever left Pembury and never went further than Tonbridge. Before she enters Foxe's pages, her life is almost entirely contained between her home and the local market. She is as close to middle-class housewife as you are likely to find in the 16th century and markedly different from her predecessors Anne Askew and Joan Bocher, both movers and shakers in the world of religion. Nevertheless she tells her neighbours that she is not prepared to go to Mass because she can find no trace of it in the Bible and does not understand it.

This is pure Protestant logic, containing the twin pillars of scriptural precedence and the priority of reason. It is the heart of the pushback against the excesses of mediaeval Church and the underpinning of the drive for both liturgy and Scripture to be in the vernacular. If it is not to be found within the pages of the Bible, and if it is not rationally coherent and comprehensible, then it is False Religion.[1] Foxe tells us that under interrogation by the Bishop of Rochester, Maurice Griffith[2], Polley "neither allowed the deitie of this sacrament, nor the absurdity of their masse."

Come her execution on 18 July 1555, Polley — like our virgins in chapter 9 — replaces her domestic obligations with the nuptials of heaven. Surrounded by a crowd so big that farmers brought cart-loads of produce to sell, she commends her fellow martyr, Wade, on his new shirt, given to him by his wife for him to die in. She describes it as his wedding shirt, and says that the huge crowd is there to celebrate his marriage. She is deploying, as Foxe does, the analogy of the early Church that martyrs were ikonic of the Bride of Christ. The notion is sufficiently encouraging that they are motivated to sing psalms on their way to the pyre.

Similarly, **Joan Beach** of Tonbridge, arrested with John Harpole, steadfastly refuses to recant under Griffith's interrogation. She articulately maintains her position, that she believes,

---

[1] I'm not entirely sure how this was squared with doctrines like the Trinity and the dual nature of the Second Person, but it was intended to make people responsible for their own religion and to give people the tools to exercise that responsibility.

[2] also known as Maurice Griffin, because this kind of happy-go-lucky approach to names isn't exclusive to women.

> "the Sacrament of the Aultare under fourmes of bread and wyne, not to be the very body and bloud of Our Saviour in substance, but onely a token and remembrance of hys death to the faithful receiver; and this his body and substance is onely in heaven, and not in the Sacrament."

In response to Griffith's description of her reputation as a heretic in Tonbridge, she blithely says that she can't answer for what other people think or say. This is a woman who is sole regent of her mind, second only to God. To her, the opinion of the crowd is moot. She is burnt in Rochester with John Harpole on 1 April 1556.

Kent has an unusually high death count for the period. The south-east, generally, has much greater access to the Protestant literature and speakers from the Continent. Despite the general reluctance to execute women, we have a good half dozen female Kentish martyrs (and martyrs of Kent). As well as Bocher (see below), Polley and Beach, we have **Anne Albright, Joan Catmer, Joan Sole, and Agnes Snoth (Smith)**, who all burn together in Canterbury on 31 January 1558. They are "gospelling women" whose virtue and integrity are, according to Parsons, dangerously subverted and corrupted by "the liberty of the new gospel."

Some of these women were inheritors of the radical fervour of the 15th and 16th centuries, in which the Lollard communities were routinely hosted and supported by women. In these *conventicles*, or house churches, women read and learned passages of the new translations of the Bible, and discussed them with the other members of the Lollard community, sometimes having the authority to preach. Under the new spiritual equality and biblical literacy that they acquired under the 'new gospel' they were transformed from broodmares and domestic labour into supportive and active workers in the Lollard cells who, like the women of the early Church, visited members of the community who were in prison, raising funds for the support of them and the community.

These radical Christian communities had given women an autonomy and responsibility in their church that Christian women hadn't seen for centuries. Many refuted the mainstream assertion that some believers — men — were more priestly than others. Famous among them is **Joan Bocher**,[3] "the most notorious Anabaptist in Kent." Bocher is well born and educated, with textile wealth in one of the principal merchant families of Essex. She is connected both to Anne Askew (herself a martyr) and to Thomas Cranmer, and it is remarkable that such a well born woman dies — the first of only two Edwardian martyrs, and the only woman to die in his reign.

Bocher is born, we think, Joan Knell in the wonderfully named village of Steeple Bumstead in Essex around 1490, which seems to have been something of a Lollard stronghold. We don't know when she marries her first husband, a local textile merchant, well connected in the area, but the year that she is widowed is the year she is first arrested, in 1528. It is apparent that for some years the Lollards had been meeting in her home, where Wycliffe New Testaments were read, expounded and discussed. Throughout her career as a religious radical it's clear that she has the Bible at her figurative fingertips. Even Parsons describes her as a reader of Scripture — which begs the question, is Parsons describing her as a Lollard minister? In language that foreshadows the language of leadership in the Church of England 300 years later, the Lollards called their leaders/teachers, 'readers'. Certainly, Bocher is so well versed that when she is imprisoned for the last year of her life, she consistently defends herself against the principal clerics of the Church[4] with the passages of Scripture that she has by heart. On this first occasion, her arrest is for holding Lollard conventicles in her home. She recants with her fingers crossed, is released, and immediately resumes her Lollardy activities.

It is about this time that she starts to travel, connecting with other Lollard communities. She is brought into the industry of actively disseminating

---

[3] a.k.a. Joan Boucher, Butcher, Baron, Barnes and – as something of an outlier – Knell. She was also known as Joan Bucher of Westgate and as Joan of Kent (not to be confused with the Joan of Kent of chapter 9).
[4] (including Rochester's own Nicholas Ridley – shortly to be Bishop of London – as well as his successor in Rochester, John Scorey)

Tyndale New Testaments. In her travels she encounters the Dutch Anabaptists and takes the relatively small theological step from Lollardy (a denomination focused on Scripture, a disinclination to baptise infants, a memorialist theology of the Eucharist, and a suspicion of anything that smacked of Mariolatry) to the Anabaptist faith (a denomination focused on Scripture, a firm belief in believers' baptism, a memorialist theology of the Eucharist, and a theology of the incarnation designed to erase the significance of the role of Mary). In the late 1530s she moves to London and joins the household of Anne Askew. With her, Bocher starts smuggling Tyndale Bibles into the Court, sewn — so the story goes — into her clothes.

In 1542 she moves to Calais and marries a fairly shadowy figure by the name of either Baron or Barnes. With him she moves the following year to Frittenden in Kent, where she (but not her husband) is arrested again for heresy. She is dobbed in by a Kentish priest named John Miles, who says that she has "manifestly denied" the Sacrament "with many slanderous words." It looks like she has been fairly explicit in her views on the Eucharist — she told her interrogators "Matins and Evensong was no better than rumbling tubs, and the mass... [is] not laudable," — and her conviction is a slamdunk. Nevertheless she is offered a chance to appeal under Henry VIII's 1540 general pardon of sacramentalism. It seems unlikely that Bocher would not have understood the content of that pardon — she's an educated woman with both international and political connections, including connections with Cranmer himself — but she instead insists on appealing to an earlier pardon of Anabaptists which is specifically repealed by the 1540 document. This puts Cranmer in a quandary. It is basically 'fessing up to being an Anabaptist, when her trial was for the more minor offence of not-quite-accurate-Eucharistic theology.

This is typical. On the one hand, during this period, we see clerics deeply reluctant to convict and execute women as heretics, while on the other hand women are all but throwing themselves on the pyre. They have the same passion, the same bloody-mindedness and the same desire for the martyr's crown as the men among whom they stand and they refuse special treatment. On this occasion, Bocher gets it anyway. Bocher has clearly been shouting her mouth off in Kent, and from the looks of things arguing with her parish priest, waving a great big "look at me, I'm an Anabaptist" flag. Nevertheless, Cranmer pardons Bocher on the slightly mysterious grounds that she is a "gynteles [genteel] person."

John Miles is clearly livid, being the one who seems to have to live with her on his patch. He writes to complain, saying that she is now "free for any man to common with her." Six years later, he gets to say "I told you so," adamant that the local outbreak of Anabaptism is her fault. This is quite a claim to make in a society which generally thinks that women are irresponsible children who can't be trusted with any responsibilities beyond home and hearth. John thinks that Bocher has had a massive influence on her community, the kind that will have required public speaking and free association with men-not-her-husband (not least because her husband shuffles off his mortal coil shortly after she is released). Bocher has been public and loud and influential when she should have been quiet and meek and passive. John is not a happy man. He is not alone. In 1549 Bocher is arrested again. This time she is not released.

In this new, shiny reign of a Reformation Prince, Cranmer is disinclined to push for a heresy trial, particularly, I suspect, against someone he knows, but Bocher gives him no option. Of the four key tenants of the Anabaptist faith, two were by now uncontentious or fairly uncontentious: Biblicism and sacramentalism (which, counterintuitively, is a decidedly un-sacramentalist view of doing Church). The remaining two, however, are decidedly unpopular with the mainstream. The Anabaptists insist on believers' baptism, a doctrine which enraged not only Catholic but the mainstream Protestants of Europe (beyond all reason). Worse than this, in the eyes of the churchmen prosecuting her, is their doctrine of the incarnation, which would still be considered beyond the pale for most denominations today.

The Anabaptist doctrine of 'celestial flesh' was a reaction to the Catholic practice of devotion to the Blessed Virgin Mary that many Protestants believed was idolatry. This devotion hinged on her identity as the 'Mother of God'. The Anabaptists therefore taught that she wasn't really his Mother because Jesus did not get his humanity *from* Mary. Mary, they argued, was in no way the *origin* of the salvation which is Jesus. She was just a vessel to his newly minted, *celestially* created human flesh — a surrogate, in fact.

Bocher spots the flaw in this argument: that the very function of the title 'Mother of God' is to guarantee Jesus' humanity. The doctrine of 'celestial flesh', in separating Jesus from Mary's flesh, separates him from his essential function to be born like us, for us, by one of us. What Bocher's interrogators fail to attend to is that Bocher's theology is not 'celestial flesh'. They are too alarmed by the spread of the Anabaptist Christology to see that Bocher's teaching is an attempt to straddle the breach between the Anabaptist distrust of Mariolatry, and the fundamental Christological need for Mary's significance.

Bocher innovates, using a reading of Paul's distinguishing between the 'natural body' and the 'spiritual body' (neither of which being distinct from a person's physical body). She preaches that the incarnation is the seed not of Mary's *flesh* but of her *faith*, in which Jesus is born of Mary's 'spiritual body', ie of the seed of her redemption. It is actually an ingenious attempt to explain how a son with a sin*less* nature could be born from a woman with a sin*ful* nature, in a theological world in which sin is considered a sexually transmitted disease. It also enables Mary to be a universal prototype of every Christian, rather than fixating on her unique status as a Virgin Mother. Whether or not you agree with her, it is a brilliant piece of reasoning which she refuses to abandon in the face of a year of clerical attrition. It costs her her life, and she's executed in the spring of 1550.

All this is not to say that the only brave women in 16th century Kent were Protestants. The dissolution of the monasteries was catastrophic for the women that had populated them and was not joyously received. In the early 16th century there were nearly 900 religious houses in England alone, so that just about everyone in the country was within walking distance of a religious house. In England there were about 2000 nuns (out of a total population in England of slightly more than 3 million), with perhaps 10 times as many dependents. By now most of the Anglo-Saxon houses had either faded out of use or been translated into men's houses, but there were houses for women in Hoo, West Malling, Canterbury, Higham, Dartford as well as possibly still houses in Grain and Eastry. Higham was the first to go, under Wolsey in 1521, followed in the 30s by a rapid succession of the other smaller houses dissolved in the first wave[5]. At this stage the curtailing of the religious life was still, broadly speaking, optional. These women were given the option of moving to a larger house, and some of them may well have showed up in Malling Abbey.

The more brutal second wave ripped from these women their home, their living and their identity. There are accounts of some religious dropping dead from grief and shock within days of leaving their monastic home. While the men were released from their vows and given comfortable pensions, Henry refused to give the women permission to marry or own property, and left them on a subsistence pension (about a quarter of that of the average monk). We do not know what happened to the nuns at Malling Abbey. Five of them were still drawing their pensions in 1553. Many religious, nuns in particular, went back to the later Anglo-Saxon practice of forming informal religious communities attached to the homes of catholic sponsors.

Malling Abbey was one of the wealthier convents in the country, making the place ripe for plunder. As early as 1535 Thomas Cromwell appoints his own steward to 'take care' of the Abbey's income. **Elizabeth Rede**, the last abbess before Hilda Stewart in 1893, resigns in protest. In 1538 the King's men bring the deed of surrender to Malling Abbey for signing. These deeds were produced wholesale for religious houses to sign across the country, as one by one the monasteries and abbeys of the country were persuaded (bullied) into handing over their assets to the Crown. Many houses were also asked to sign a document renouncing their former life as superstitious and corrupt, but it looks as though Malling Abbey escaped this particular humiliation. In fact, the nuns

---

[5] when all of the houses with an income of less than £200 were closed down.

refuse to sign the Deed. Despite this remarkable protest, the prioress, Margaret Vernon (Cromwell's appointment after Rede's resignation), manages to negotiate a comfortable pension for herself and an income of sorts for the other nuns. The Abbey lands and rights become the property of Thomas Cranmer, who leases it to his brother-in-law.

This absorption of the monastic properties into the figurative pockets of the King and his mates has resulted in the general assumption that the dissolution of the monasteries was principally a financial exercise. There is, however, another likely motive in the mix: revenge. The religious houses of England represented everything that Henry's new religion wasn't, and they were loved for it. The monasteries often figured in the resistance against Henry's declaration of his own supremacy. The male houses, in particular, were more independent from the national ecclesiastical structures, and they were part of an international network during a time when Henry was trying to cut himself free from continental control. In particular, most outrageously, the monasteries disseminated the country's unease regarding the King's divorce — the monasteries, and in particular one monastery, one woman.

Around the time that Joan Bocher is being arrested for the first time as a Lollard in Essex, a young woman called **Elizabeth Barton** is entering the court of Henry VIII as a nationally proclaimed prophetess. Barton is born in about 1506 from fairly humble stock and becomes a servant in the household of Thomas Cob in Adlington. In about 1525 she develops what seems to be epilepsy, or something similar, along with a painful affliction to her throat. At the same time she starts having prophetic visions. Her first vision is apparently to predict that a child being nursed along with her was about to die, but not all of her preternatural knowledge was so awful: she also has a vision telling her what the local hermit had for dinner!

For a year or so Barton astounds the local community with her prescience and with spiritual utterings promising both the blessings of heaven for the righteous, as well as the torments of hell for unbelievers and heretics. Time and again she urges adherence to the traditional catholic disciplines of the

Mass, pilgrimage and penance. Her reputation grows until in 1526 her parish priest, Richard Masters[6], contacts the Archbishop of Canterbury, William Warham, who sends a commission to investigate. The commission arrives, led by the examiner, a Canterbury monk called Edward Bocking. Bocking declares her genuine — pious, informed and orthodox. He writes his report for Henry VIII, who palms it off onto Thomas More, who in turn is carefully long-armed in his opinion.

Then, still in 1526, she has a vision of the Virgin Mary telling her that the Holy Virgin has herself rescued Barton from death. Barton is sent by the Virgin to a nearby chapel at Court-at-Street[7] to be healed. Given Barton's tendency to hook her visitations to feasts of the Virgin, it's likely it was Lady Day (25th March). Apparently the nearby streets were lined by thousands of people wanting to witness the miracle. Barton prostrates herself in the chapel, and afterwards declares herself to be healed. (It is unclear whether or not she actually is.)

On the back of this Barton has another vision of the Virgin Mary telling her to commit herself to the religious life in honour of the Virgin. This vision also specifies Bocking as her confessor: a stipulation which needs to be ratified by the Archbishop, which it duly is. Her visions thus far are written up[8] by Edward Thwaites, a local Justice of the Peace connected to the then Archbishop of Canterbury. This pamphlet continues to circulate the country for the rest of Barton's unnaturally shortened life. The chapel at Court-at-Street becomes a place of pilgrimage, where miraculous healings continue to be reported.

Once she moves to the convent in Canterbury, St Sepulchre's, she encounters the revelations of Bridget

---

[6] It's worth noting that Aldington defeats the stereotype of the ignorant medieval priest. They have a tendency to appoint thoroughly educated scholars – Master's predecessor was Erasmus (yes, *that* Erasmus) and Masters is by no means a fool. He nevertheless swings at Tyburn for his involvement with Barton.
[7] "... *it is a view to cross yourself at: vast, misty, silver, melancholy, exhilarating, incredibly romantic at almost any time of year.*" Alan Neame
[8] "A Marvellous Work of late done at Court-of-Street in Kent and published to the devout People of this time for their spiritual consolation." (1527 – a time when a title wasn't expected to be pithy.)

of Sweden and Catherine of Siena, two saints famous for their prophetic visions and for their — and this is important — habit of rebuking kings and popes. Then, in 1527 Henry VIII declares his intention to reorder his marital affairs. Barton's visions become distinctly political. As her influence is becoming national, her revelations are being shared with religious houses around the country, especially the renown Syon Abbey. Archbishop Warham writes a letter of recommendation to Cardinal Wolsey, who introduces her to the King and gets her a face-to-face.

With unbelievable fearlessness, Barton tells Henry that his proposed marriage is an affront to God and his Church. He must, she says, restore orthodoxy and eschew Anne Boleyn. She continues abroad in the same themes, preaching some serious hell-fire in the King's direction. Across the country her pamphlets travel, often copied and disseminated by other monasteries (Syon, again), announcing that the King's divorce was a thing of wickedness, that anyone who assists him is damned, and that the King himself would be damned and dethroned, and the country ruined, if he goes through with the divorce. She pulls no punches, makes no allowances for psychopathic monarchical privilege.

Barton appears to be articulating the widespread fear of Henry's policies, perhaps particularly among religious houses who are looking at the rhetoric coming out of London with some apprehension. Certainly there is popular expectation that the split with Rome will spell disaster for England. Barton's predictions of war, plague, and the overthrowing of the kingdom voice common fears. Before long there is a steady queue of people asking Barton for her opinion on a wide range of matters, but particularly regarding the King's divorce. Sir Thomas More, one of her adherents and not a fool, tries to dissuade her from responding, but she will not. As well as widespread popular appeal, she also has powerful friends, including the Bishop of Rochester, John Fisher. As Henry leans further towards Protestantism, Barton continually urges orthodoxy and papal supremacy.

Initially, Henry tries the diplomatic path, offering to make her an abbess. Similarly, his fiancée, Anne Boleyn, invites her to come and be part of her entourage at court. Then, in 1533, Henry marries Anne and Barton starts touting a divinely elected successor (the Marquees of Exeter) to the ungodly King. She sends messages to Rome urging the Pope to condemn Henry and messages are sent to the Holy Roman Emperor, connecting John Fisher, Bishop of Rochester, to Barton's call for invasion and godly rule. Worst of all, from Henry's point of view, Barton prophesies that he will lose his throne within a month of his marriage to Anne. Within striking distance of that month (from the public announcement of the marriage) Pope Clement VII provisionally excommunicates Henry, effectively declaring open season on his throne.

In what may have been the last straw for the King, Barton arranges several simultaneous sermons against his actions and policies. Interestingly, for those convinced that she was just a pawn, she insists that her preachers undergo significant penance — hair shirts and the like — before this takes place. Henry's approach shifts from diplomacy to force.

In August 1533 the newly enthroned Archbishop Cranmer, armed with Cromwell's intelligence, conducts a series of interviews with Barton at Otford. On 11 August, Barton requests a trip to her shrine at Court-at-Street, in the hope of getting a vision for the feast of the Assumption. In September, after the birth of Princess Elizabeth leaves Henry increasingly vulnerable in his lack of male heirs, Cromwell and Cranmer renew their attack. This time they are joined by Hugh Latimer[9], who is manifestly unsympathetic.

Here the story divides. In the state version, it is Latimer who tricks her into a betrayal of ignorance, which her accusers say proves that she was never a prophetess. The young woman, not yet out of her 20s, stripped of her defenders and alone against three of the sharpest minds in the country, collapses. Richard Morrison, not a friendly witness, describes her confessing to a ruse created "to satisfy the minds of them which resorted unto her, and to obtain worldly praise."

---

[9] Bishop of Worcester, who is, as it happens, martyred himself, later in this merry-go-round of orthodoxy that is Tudor England.

In another telling, Barton's recantation is an act of faith, lining herself up for the martyr's death she knows is hers. It buys time for her supporters to organise. It puts her in the Star Chamber to witness to her vision.

Barton recants, however, not just once, but twice, and her reputation does not survive it.

Everyone associated with her is also arrested and in November her reputation is publicly trashed. She is denounced across the country, and has to undergo penance in London and then in the precincts of Canterbury Cathedral. While she's humiliated, a sermon[10] is preached against her both in the Precincts and in London. The Act of Attainder[11] (the declaration of her guilt) accusing her of treason is published and distributed across the country. In it all speech defending her is forbidden and it demands the surrender of any texts concerning her. So successful is this purge, that there are no extant copies of any of the very many publications of her miracles or revelations. Barton is transformed from 'The Holy Maid of Kent' to 'The Mad Maid of Kent.' On 20 April 1534 — the day all Londoners had to swear the Oath of Succession — Barton dies a traitor's death with the men that supported her. Such is the King's wrath, that rather than being burnt as was normally the case for female traitors, Barton is sentenced to be hung, drawn and quartered: publicly humiliated, dismembered and broken. She is the only woman to have had her head put on a spike at London Bridge.

The total defacing of her memory indicates that Barton is more than a pawn, that there is more to her than a mere footnote in the story of the King's Great Matter. Cranmer himself in his own private correspondence writes, "*And truly, I think, she did marvellously stop the going forward of the King's marriage by the reasons of her visions ...*" I suspect that the support she had across the country,

---

[10] "The Sermon against the Holy Maid of Kent and Her Adherents" 1533 – unlike the Maid's own words, we have a good record of this particular document: the state's last word against her.

[11] "*An Act concerning the Attainder of Elizabeth Barton and others*" This, itself, is extremely contentious. An Act of Attainder was a device to circumnavigate the courts, but this one omits all reference to any actual grounds for treason (ie her support of the Marquees of Exeter) and is more like an accusation of heresy. Cue lots of legal sucking in of teeth.

particularly among the religious houses and catholic-leaning clergy, was such that she came very close to derailing the whole thing. More and Fisher did not survive association with her and there is evidence that, despite their backpedalling, communities like Syon Abbey never quite shook off the taint. Barton herself has to be utterly obliterated from the public record, so powerful are her words. If we compare her to those other prophetesses — Hildegard, Katharine, Bridget — and see the impact that they made on their contemporaries, we can see why only total annihilation was enough.

In fact, in many ways, Barton's witness feels like the dying breath of mediaeval spirituality in England. Point for point, she is analogous to other, broadly contemporaneous women across Europe, who used the pattern of self-abnegation to amplify their vision. Hildegard, Catherine, Bridget, and a host of women through the Middle Ages, used the role of the prophetess to speak truth to power and to call their peers to repentance and revival. It is even typical that this prophecy is accompanied by illness: it played into the tropes of female frailty and physicality. As women were generally considered unfit for the spiritual life because of their overwhelming physicality, in these women the womanly body was overwhelmed by the things of heaven. As with Foxe's martyrs, the prophetess' inferiority was understood to underline the profundity of her vision (words "so holy and wise" could not possibly be the simple pronouncements of a devout woman, natch).

The only difference is the overwhelming pride of the man to whom she addressed her campaign. The reason she is not remembered with the likes of Bridget of Sweden is not because she was less committed or devout — to the contrary, all the evidence we have points to her being genuine, intelligent and pious, convincing the vast majority of those who heard her. Rather, the massive propaganda campaign that followed her death systematically and efficiently destroyed her reputation. Her memory is overwritten with satire and mockery. Cruel parodies cast her as lascivious, mad, bad: frail like all her sex, and deluded and misled by wicked men. Only her recantation is recorded for posterity, not her visions, and, scandalously, we have believed the rewrite.

Instead, what we see with Elizabeth Barton is the closing of the door to one of the few avenues to power for women, other than blood and marriage: the prophetess. We haven't seen her like since. A generally accepted prophetess had real power in mediaeval Europe in a way we have largely forgotten. Over the centuries, as the idea of Barton being a simple pawn won out over the memory of her influence, so faded also out of view the story of her being lascivious. In this successful recasting of Barton as a powerless, misled woman, we can still see the relationship between women's power and their bodies.

Prophets, rebels and witnesses, the women of this chapter refused to be put in the token box of their sex. They refused to be told what they should believe, and how they should express their faith. When they were overcome by the power of the establishment, it did not diminish what they stood for. Even the nuns of Malling Abbey, whose voice we don't have and whose protest wasn't recorded, left a mark in the silence of their dissent. They should not be forgotten.

Both Bocher and Barton were hugely influential on either side of the same battlefield. (They were so nearly contemporaries, it's fun to try and imagine them in conversation, although it would have been quite explosive!) Bocher was too far beyond the theological pale to be recorded by Foxe, but she was working at a perfectly orthodox (Protestant) problem: the matter of properly acknowledging the incarnation without excessively elevating Mary. By many measures, hers was less problematic than the modern Protestant solution of transforming Mary into an entirely passive host. Conversely, Barton *was* orthodox, and on a par with many women whom we now call saints. Her (male) contemporaries on the losing side, Fisher and More, are remembered with honour, yet her memory was deliberately maligned, stamped out and effaced as a warning against presumptuous women who challenge the establishment.

In fact not *one single female Reformation martyr* is commemorated by name by the Church of England[12], despite the shocking numbers of women on both sides

---

[12] I owe this unedifying discovery to my son.

who were convinced that their faith was more important than their family, their reputation or their lives. I'm not sure whether they are considered insufficiently holy, or merely uninspiring. All I can say is that their contemporaries thought otherwise.

Women in power

People don't get into the calendar of saints for their ability to change things using mechanisms of power. Neither Thomas nor Oliver Cromwell, for example, make it in, despite their genuinely devout reforming zeal. Anthony Cooper gets in, granted, but as a social reformer, rather than politician — and he is, at least, a peer of the realm who thus had the good grace to *inherit* his authority. Anthony aside, all the people celebrated by the Church of England for wielding political power are royal — which says some extremely interesting things about the Church of England. It strongly indicates that power is only considered acceptable if you acquire it by an accident of birth. There is more than a suggestion that seeking political power to accomplish a goal, even one formed by faith and Christian ideals, does not, as the book[1] has it, "excite people to holiness." This is a limitation to holiness that invites question, an opinion of 'dirty politics' that is a self-fulfilling prophecy.[2] We should celebrate politicians with integrity all the more when it is a treacherous path to tread.

Identifying motives, of course, is never easy, especially in a society in which the language and habits of religion formed part of the current culture. It's even harder for the women who have achieved power. A man like Cromwell could rise through his merits and connections, but for women, politically, the only route to power, for centuries, was through blood and/or sex — and even blood wasn't that reliable. Those who managed to marry well and to a man open to influence had to be careful how they portrayed themselves if they were to avoid all the knee-jerk tropes and hostilities. Often, those women who have not been written into passivity, are similarly translucent

---

[1] *Exciting Holiness: Collects and Readings for the Festivals and Lesser Festivals of the Calendars of the Church of England, the Church of Ireland, the Scottish Episcopal Church and the Church in Wales*
[2] Labelling politics as 'dishonourable' inevitably discourages honourable people.

because they have kept their motives, and the degree of influence over the men around them, discreet. They had good reason.

One of the persistent tropes of the misogynist playbook is of the power-hungry whore. As we saw in the last chapter, a powerful, influential or transgressive woman is constantly at risk of being painted as an out-of-control-woman, in lurid shades of sexual immorality. In the stories of **Anne Boleyn**, *Queen*, the suggestion that she might have been a scheming hussy is stuck to her more tightly than her title.

This is manifestly unfair. For starters, there is every evidence that Boleyn's relationship with Henry was a genuine romance, not a cold-blooded seduction. Not only is there all the skipping-through-the-daisies of their public life, but her highly emotional reaction to the Seymour affair argues for a less than calculating nature. Court opinion at the time was very clear:
A) challenging the king's behaviour was unwise;
B) forcing Henry to choose between her or Seymour put her on the same footing as the mistress.
She does so, it is reasonable to conclude, because hers is a romance, and the emotional relationship was her principal credibility. It is not this rivalry that kills her, though, it merely creates a weak flank on which she could be brought down — and, for historians, a satisfying frame within which to contain her story.

Boleyn is, rather, a woman of significant integrity and faith whose story could have sat in a number of different chapters in this book, not least the one preceding. She is a patron and also a martyr, arguably, who locked horns with men of power. She is a scholar, too, but her influence in the English Reformation led me to include her here, as a woman in power: Boleyn is born and formed to be a courtier — to live and thrive at the cutting-edge of power and policy (literally, alas, in her case).

She is evidently a woman of deep personal faith. None of the descriptions of her as flirtatious, bad-tempered, as a scheming politician or a patron of her friends undermine the sincerity of her faith or the significance of her contribution to the English Reformation. "*If political acumen, wit and enjoyment of the good things of life were incompatible with religious fervour then King David would be on the same footing as Ahab.*" (William Marshall) As I say, it is arguable that her faith is what killed her. What goes wrong for Boleyn is that she clashes with the other significant machinator in the court, Thomas Cromwell, and clashes with him over a matter of conscience.

Anne Boleyn is born in the first decade of the 16th century. Rumour has it she's born in Norfolk, but it is a rumour we will stoutly ignore in preference of the tradition that she is born at Hever Castle. Born there or not, however, Hever was owned by the Boleyns and it houses prayer books[3] annotated by Boleyn in her youth. For sure, much of Henry's courtship of Boleyn takes place at Hever. She is, undoubtedly, a Kentish Maid ... or possibly a maid of Kent. Made in Kent, anyway.

As was still the practice in the Early Modern nobility, Boleyn's political training begins while she's still a child, when she is sent to another household. In this case, to live at the court of Margaret of Austria, Catherine of Aragon's sister-in-law, and Renaissance Regent in the Netherlands. There, she sees what it looks like to be a Renaissance Queen and it's likely Boleyn models herself on this influential and powerful woman. While Margaret remains a Catholic all her life, she is, in the broadest sense of the word, a liberal. She is certainly a humanist[4] and encourages a great range of thinkers and theologians in her court. The young Boleyn is therefore surrounded by earnest and devout people grappling with the principal issue of the day: the flood of religious contention spilling out of the Lutheran cauldron in Germany. Margaret's court is full of visiting thinkers, where preachers and religious speakers draw crowds and comment. Like Brexit, or whether dogs are better than cats (they are), almost no one is neutral, and Boleyn clearly lands on the Protestant side of the debate.

On Boleyn's bookshelf, only the oldest books are in Latin, and the rest is a library of evangelical works. Once in the English Court, she is known to smuggle in more radical books under the counter, as it were, via her silk woman

---

[3] Subsequently carefully curated and handed down the female line

[4] "... humanism called for the comprehensive reform of culture, the transfiguration of what humanists termed the passive and ignorant society of the "dark" ages into a new order that would reflect and encourage the grandest human potentialities." (Britanica) Basically they were the humanities students who provided the intellectual drive behind the Renaissance.
Never let it be said that the humanities are irrelevant.

(i.e. purveyor of silk) Joan Wilkinson.[5] This isn't to say that there was no trace of the Old Religion in her spirituality. A prototype of the Church of England, deep roots of Catholicism are still visible in her devotion to the Eucharist. She refuses to have Tristram Revell's translation of *Farrago Rerum Theologicarum* dedicated to her, it's assumed, because of its denial of the Real Presence. She spends her last night on Earth praying before the reserved Sacrament. In essence, however, she becomes a Reformer, and she throws herself into the work with a will.

Boleyn is known to support scholars at Oxbridge and abroad in Paris and Padua. Her biographer, Latymer[6], records that she persuades Henry to exempt universities from the clerical tax which was costing other clergy 10% of their income. She founds schools and is heavily involved in the reform and reorganisation of the universities. This is no nominal Christian. Even her enemies acknowledge that she is "a favorer of Gods worde". When there was not a little risk in acknowledging it, Cranmer's still writes to Henry on hearing the news of Boleyn's arrest, "I loved her not a little for the love which I judged her to bear toward God and his gospel."

The younger Boleyn girl is a humanist, like her role-model, putting considerable effort into both poor relief and educational patronage. She employs her own almoner whose task it is to identify individuals that need assistance, and she spends considerable sums providing clothes, livestock and alms to the poorer communities around her. (Foxe records eye-watering amounts spent on poor relief, but if you dock a zero it becomes plausible, but still considerable, and also matches corroborating evidence, suggesting a typo that the hagiographer didn't bother to correct.)

In all this Boleyn manifestly has a considerable influence on her fiancé/husband. Cranmer writes to Henry that he is sure that "your Grace's favour to the gospel was not made by affection unto her, but zeal..." Writing as he is after Boleyn's arrest it carries something of an air of excessive protest. Henry's theology shifts quite

---

[5] Who, btw, gets her own reference in Foxe's *Martyrs*.
[6] There are two Latimers in Boleyn's story, both of whom spent time as her chaplain, which must've been confusing. (It was to me, anyway.) Her biographer sometimes has his name spelt with a Y, which I have used, to distinguish him from Hugh Latimer, bishop and martyr.

significantly in the 10 years or so of their relationship. For example, Boleyn is reputed to be the one who put the incendiary document *Supplication for the Beggars* in front of Henry, a document that proved influential in Henry's actions against the Church and the monasteries in particular. It was to Boleyn that the author's wife appealed for protection against the wrath of Thomas More and for her husband's access to the King — access that was granted. Friends of another benighted reformer, Patmore, also applied to Boleyn for help with his cause, clearly conscious of her influence.

It is not just Henry's theology we can attribute to Boleyn, but the influence of Cranmer and a number of other key Reformers. Cranmer, for example — one of the principal figures of the English Reformation, is her protégé. He is sent to live with the Boleyns while he writes his treatise in defence of the King's Cause. At this point in his story he is a minor academic, of no particular interest. Boleyn promotes Cranmer as her household chaplain and Henry himself credits Cranmer's later elevation to Canterbury to Boleyn. The promotion of her chaplain, Latimer (bishop and martyr) and her almoner, Shaxton, to significant bishoprics also have her hand behind them. She does a sizable amount to populate both the Court and the Bench of Bishops with reformers, in fact.

At the time of the notorious breach with Cromwell, the legislation to close down the smaller monasteries and subsume their wealth into the Royal purse was awaiting Royal assent. Boleyn and her reformers want the monastic money to be kept to its intended purpose, Boleyn's twin passions of education and poor relief, in line with Wolsey's earlier Reforms. Cromwell, on the other hand, has an eye on gaping holes in the Crown's finances. The subsequent fight will kill the young queen.

Boleyn recruits Latimer and possibly Cranmer to preach on the subject of how-monasteries-should-be-converted-to-places-of-study, or, at least, that their funds should be diverted for the relief of the poor. Her biographer records a delegation of monastics calling on the Queen for her protection, so it seems she's made waves the monastics thought were hopeful. As Latymer describes it, Boleyn rebukes them for their corruptions but hears their promises of reform. Certainly the bill was passed with a clause allowing exceptions. There's a good argument to be made that it is Boleyn's influence that creates it. If

Latymer is right, she seems set to create as many exceptions as possible, funnelling much of the funds into education.

On Passion Sunday, 2nd April 1536, a month to the day before Boleyn is arrested, her chaplain John Skip preaches a passionate (if not beautifully formed) sermon against malicious attacks against the clergy and the monasteries, wicked Royal advisers and the folly of avarice. It is a gauntlet thrown down in a challenge that Boleyn loses. While there is no doubt that there were a number of other factors in her death, and the involvement of her husband is hotly debated, when examining motive, *follow the money* is something of an axiom. This is an argument over money, over principle versus pragmatism, and neither can afford to lose.

Boleyn and Cromwell had been allies, and powerful ones at that. When they fall out it is unlikely that the loser is going to be allowed to continue to have any influence. Neither can allow the other to remain in Court queering the pitch — all their people, all their mechanisms are the same. Boleyn has considerable international influence, too, with ambassadors and diplomats courting her as Queen, and as a patron in her own right. When she falls out with Cromwell, Boleyn's influence has to be excised completely. And it isn't like she can be fired — you only have to look at the impact of Catherine of Aragon[7] on English politics to see the influence an exiled Queen can have without even trying.

Cranmer's victory in the short battle is swift and absolute. On the morning of 19th May 1536, Boleyn is led out to the scaffold to die. She wears crimson — a clear statement that she considers she has a claim to a martyr's crown. Her last words are, according to the majority of witnesses, "Jesu receive my soul."

In 1559, 23 years later, the to-be-Bishop-of-London, John Aylmer (not an entirely disinterested historian) describes Boleyn as "the chief, first and only cause of banyshing the beast of Rome." John Foxe adds that she is "a zelous defender ... of Christes gospel," optimistically concluding that "all the world doth know and her acts doe and will declare to the worldes ende." In short, it is a mystery to me that Edward and Charles are both described as 'King

---

[7] Henry VIII's first wife (divorced wife no.1)

and martyr' with much more tenuous claims to martyrdom than Anne Boleyn, and much lighter impacts on the spiritual life of the country. Boleyn's is not a parallel story to Howard.[8] Boleyn is one of the principal influences of the Reformation, surrounding Henry VIII with reformers and with reforming ideas and literature. She impacts legislation, and — to her near contemporaries — she's Peak Renaissance, and an equivalent of her stepson, Edward.

Her redrafting as a 'wronged woman'/scheming floozy mirrors Barton's. Like the prophetess, Boleyn's story has been retold as that of the object of other men's machinations rather than as a politician in her own right. Thus reworked, the most important thing about her is safely restored to matters of her body — whether or not she can reproduce, and with whom she is having sex — rather than what she has *done*. In life her power is excised by physical erasure; in death she is neutered by a sort of national amnesia. We have deliberately forgotten who she was: Queen, Philanthropist and Reformer.

Eleanor Plantagenet's story is very different. It ends better, insofar as she doesn't die a violent death, and the civil war that she is part of results in a precedent for the House of Commons and the beginnings of representative democracy. However, she is very rarely included in the story.

Eleanor's birth is not recorded, but being King John's youngest child she could not have been born much after 1215. Her mother, who had been kept on a tight rein by King John, heads back to her family in France shortly after Eleanor's birth. The Plantagenet children are separated and Eleanor is brought up by de Roches, a crusader and the Bishop of Winchester. She is well educated, the better to equip her for a life of devotion/the running of a household/convent. We know that her governess taught Eleanor to read and write in English, French and Latin. As a noblewoman, Eleanor's childhood is setting her up for one of the two fates available to her: mother or nun.

As it happens, Eleanor does both twice over. Firstly she is married at the — even for her times — scandalously young age of nine years old. This first marriage to the second William Marshall (the son of the man who fought off the

---

[8] Henry VIII's fifth wife (executed wife no.2)

first Barons' Rebellion in 1217) ends when she is widowed at about 16. After which she made a decidedly interesting oath of celibacy.

None of the historians seem to think that this was caused by being married to a man in his 30s when she was nine (but I'm just going to leave the thought there). The usual interpretation is that it gives her an edge in what becomes a lifelong campaign to get back her dower which the Marshall family refuses to pay. Her attempts to retrieve what is due are an ongoing theme for the rest of her life. It is worth a considerable sum of money, so her celibacy may well be intended to reassure the Marshalls that the dower lands would not be lost to the family in a second marriage.

It is also possible that it is inspired by teenage fervour. Her foster father is not only the Bishop of one of the principal sees, but a crusading one at that. I mean, literally, got on a horse and rode to Jerusalem, wielding a sword. The fact that she goes on to break her oath to marry another crusader suggests that this left an impression on the young Princess. Her governess, too, is a famously pious and literate woman (she successfully foils an assassination attempt because she had stayed up to read her Psalter). Also in Eleanor's household is another devout woman, Cecily of Sandford. Under their combined influence, Eleanor visits a number of religious houses whilst a widow. Cecily is sufficiently invested that she takes the oath of celibacy with her. Eleanor also corresponds with the friars she has met growing up, in particular Adam Marsh. This last correspondence continues throughout her adult life, and the letters we have from Adam assume on her part biblical literacy and devotion. They indicate sufficient intimacy for the friar to criticise the princess' temper and vanity. Even if her motives for the oath are mixed, then, we can be confident that as an oath it is sincere.

Nevertheless, however fervent her religion at 16, it is no match for her passions at 26. In 1229, Simon de Montfort arrives in England, speaking only French, with a reputation as a fearsome crusader and an ambition to be Earl of Leicester. He proper sweeps Eleanor off her feet and they have what is heavily implied to be a shotgun wedding in the chapel of Eleanor's royal brother, Henry III. Eleanor's new husband does a pilgrimage by way of penance (this apparently made marrying a woman sworn to celibacy okay) and then sets out with his wife to make a string of babies over the next 20 years. Oh, and also to start a war with her brother in an attempt to create representative democracy.

Like most civil wars, the Second Barons' War is a complicated hotch potch of personal relationships failing, individual ambitions and high principle. On the one hand we have the running sore of money troubles and debt between the de Montforts and the King. Then we have Henry's desire for military glory, for which he really is incompetent. The resulting baronial grievance builds as Henry persists in taxing his country for funds to run military campaigns that everybody knows he's going to lose. Lastly, we have the King's rejection of the Magna Carta. This document is still shiny and new, forged after the First Barons' War against Henry's father, John, but Henry is honouring it more in the breach than in the keeping of it. Not only is he trying to raise taxes without the consultation enshrined in the Carta, but he's letting his friends run amok and local officials are still unfettered. From town councils through to the Crown, power is still unaccountable, and a number of people are unhappy about it.

The Second Barons' War is more than just a power struggle for the de Montforts. Firstly, de Montfort is a crusader, a man of conviction, not inclined to half measures[9]. God is on the battlefield and next to his skin.[10] For de Montfort, the schemes of polecats and of people are all part of the economy of God. When he extracts the Provisions of Oxford[11] out of Henry III, de Montfort insists that everybody takes an oath to uphold the provisions. Whatever anybody else is thinking, de Montfort spends the night in prayer and fasting. His oath is binding. His principles are unyielding. Before his battles with Henry III,

---

[9] There are some concerning tendencies to anti-Semitism that emerge as Simon de Montfort gains power, and the attack on the London Jews unsettled even his contemporaries. I would tentatively suggest that perhaps being brought up to solve religious disputes by force, even crossing continents to do so, sets a poor standard for tolerance.
[10] (he wears a hair-shirt)
[11] "The 'Provisions of Oxford' placed the king under the authority of a Council of Fifteen, to be chosen by twenty-four men made up of twelve nominees of the king, and twelve nominees of the reformers. The chief ministers, the Justiciar and Chancellor were to be chosen by and responsible to the Council of Fifteen, and ultimately to the community of the realm at regular parliaments to be held three times a year." (Parliament.uk)

de Montfort brings his supporting bishops in to bless the troops. He conducts this war like a crusade.

Eleanor, too, has every sign of being a woman of principle, with a slice of obsession. Despite consistently struggling to make ends meet, she is organising the patronage of a number of houses of mendicant orders, as well as supporting the Cistercian Abbey in Waverley and the Benedictine Abbey in St Albans. Wherever she travels she takes trusted clerics with her, and she's known to advise her husband, taking in turn advice from a small group of spiritual counsellors like Adam Marsh and Gregory de Bosellis. Long before civil war breaks out in 1264, Eleanor is advocating on behalf of members of her household — which for a Countess in the 13th century can be a group of people numbering into the hundreds — who have been caught up in Henry's edicts.

De Montfort's reforms are about more than just condensing power around people like him. The Provisions of Oxford establish the first Parliament meeting independently of the King, meeting to consider wider matters than simply taxation, made up not just of barons but of knights and burgesses — it's a real game changer with real distribution of power. Even though, in the end, de Montfort is literally butchered, and the Provisions unpicked, the precedent remains. This is not just about the money, this is a crusade for liberty and the restriction of autocracy. The rebels under de Montfort conduct the most significant reforms of the English constitution until the 1640s.

This is not Simon's fight alone. He has a vital ally at his back — his wife and councillor. We have Eleanor Plantagenet's household accounts from 1265. Along with other correspondence from the time, they show that Eleanor takes a pivotal role as director of communications during the civil war. The war breaks out in 1264, when Henry refuses to abide by the Provisions of Oxford. As de Montfort's fortunes wax and wane Eleanor is the one who keeps communications flowing between her husband and her sons, spread out as they are across the south of England. While her husband is in the ascendancy, it is Eleanor who is responsible for most of the Royal hostages. She is also a diplomatic point for friends, allies and potential allies. During the early part of 1265 she receives more than 50 visitors from among their baronial and religious connections. These connections are not irrelevant when it comes to extricating her family from the disaster of Evesham.

The turning point for the de Montforts is the escape of the Crown Prince, Edward, from Hereford. Not a fool, Eleanor hotfoots it to Dover where she prepares for siege. There, she buys weapons and stone, and employs a master engineer as well as stonemasons to improve the defences. She continues her diplomatic efforts rallying as much support as she can for her husband and her sons. Then in August 1265, Edward's forces meet de Montfort's at Evesham. It is a testament to the radicalism of de Montfort's reforms that his defeat is not enough. Edward sends a death squad to hunt de Montfort down on the battlefield and butcher him. Chroniclers of the time described it as murder. It is the first time a nobleman is deliberately cut down in battle and it spells the beginning of the end of the age of chivalry.

Eleanor is knocked sideways. Even in the middle of the siege preparations, she withdraws for over a week and emerges subdued — subdued, but not overcome. When Edward arrives with his army, she is ready. Her fellow widow and ally, Aline Basset, surrenders her husband's stronghold in London immediately, but Eleanor has terms she wants met. Eleanor holds Dover until she has obtained the safety of her substantial household — and smuggled her surviving sons to safety onto the continent. That achieved, she withdraws to France. She retires to a Dominican convent, a cloistered order, where she spends the remaining decade of her life. (She is still pursuing the matter of the dowry from her first marriage, unresolved after all this time.)

The household roll of 1265 completes the picture of a woman who is at once political and domestic, devout and conniving. It records the money spent ordering a new book of hours for her daughter, arranging pilgrimage for one of her ladies even while she's retreating from Edward's army. She employs several chaplains across her estates as well as an almoner to organise poor relief. This relief is more than token. There is a generous sum set aside for the daily relief of the poor, as well as those that she takes in to feed at her table. The household roll lists the comings and goings of the allies and spiritual support, both, who are regularly visiting her. It records the changing of her diet, almsgiving and clothing after the death of her husband, and also the day-to-day devotions and charities that the de Montfort estates deploys.

Eleanor's faith, her politics and her family life are all intertwined. There is no line to be drawn that divides for her where family is separate from politics, and politics from faith. The campaign that she and her husband wage, for the diffusion of power and the representation of ordinary people, is so radical that time and again Henry III is able to renege on his obligations with the support of popes and kings, but they persist. They succeed in creating, however briefly, a form of representational government that is unique in Europe for centuries.

Anne Boleyn and Eleanor Plantagenet are examples of women of faith who have had significant impact on the political and religious history of our nation. They are a shape of woman who is scarcely researched and hard to quantify: their husband's viceroy and councillor.[12] Certainly, few men were saying much about it at the time. The likes of Eleanor are largely forgotten while others, like Boleyn, have been significantly shrunk and maligned in their retelling. They both deserve to be remembered for the people of power and influence that they were. We could do worse than reminding ourselves of the women who have had a vision of a different country and pulled on all the levers at their disposal in order to move it closer. In fact, we do well to celebrate those who have used political power for the common good. Faith and politics absolutely should mix, as well for women as for men.

---

[12] Cf chapter 9

Patrons

It was expected for women of power and influence to be patrons. Both Eleanor and Boleyn were substantial patrons of churches and individuals, for example. Until Adam Smith, the accumulation of wealth was considered spiritually problematic: the wealth you had constituted resources someone else did not have. A wealthy person, in other words, had an unfair slice of the pie. A system of spiritual money laundering was inevitable. Wealth needed to be offset with charity and patronage. Moreover, a huge infrastructure of scholars, priests and religious running a network of, in effect, libraries, schools, hospitals and hostels, food banks, therapy and art galleries, required a steady income from patrons. I say this not to diminish the worship that took place in these institutions, but because this religion of the word needed a lot of resources to be translated into action and understanding in an unlettered era. It was in the Church's interest to encourage vicarious participation from those not actively engaged.

But there's more to it than this. While the quote is, *where your treasure is, there your heart will be also,* this statement is reversible. A good guide to someone's priorities is to look at where they're spending their money. Theology and anthropology both will lead you to the conclusion that people put their resources towards the things they consider important. Thus in the codified world of the Middle Ages, patronage and charity were necessary prerequisites for salvation, while after the Reformation, they were symptoms of it.

Unimagined by historians, and generally un-remembered by the people and institutions that they empowered, are the women who made a significant impact in this respect (albeit most of them not on the scale of queens and countesses). Their giving was often restricted by their limited control of their resources. Married women's action and property were often concealed under the identity of the husband — as we saw with Eleanor Plantagenet. Byrhtric is recorded as having made a substantial donation to Rochester Cathedral 'with his wife' Aelfswith. How involved in that donation she was, we can never know.

Widows and unmarried women were often vulnerable to predation and poverty — so few women remained single for long. Until the Reformation, at least, unmarried women out of childhood and not under vows were rare. Even under these limitations, women still gave, although the gifts were often practical: food, linen, jewellery. The archives of the country are full of wills leaving bequests to religious organisations and people. The majority of these show that women were regularly supporting people to whom they are connected by politics, friendship or kinship. It's noticeable that often the bequests of women are of the only things they had control of: their own personal possessions. It's not an unreasonable extension to this to conceive of similar gifts in their lifetime, perhaps on a visit. Such gifts in kind would be unlikely to be recorded.

In 1522, for example, **Margery Sandes**, the sister of two of the nuns at Malling Abbey, requests in her will that she might be buried in the Abbey Church. Alongside this request she leaves her wedding ring for the crucifix at the altar where women sought divine help — or the help of the saints (most likely St Margaret) — for childbirth. She also left her bedding to the abbess and sundry other cushions and covers to the other nuns including, "*to be divided among the nuns where there was most need: six pillows, 11 pairs of sheets, four tablecloths, the curtain and all her brass and pewter ware*." Sandes is a widow, and probably childless, because she also had the resources — and the control of her funds — to leave 20 shillings for the high altar and an annuity of 20 ½ shillings a year intended for the next 20 years. (Before the annuity had run out, the Abbey would be closed and its resources 'privatised'.)

Some of the traces of the patronesses of Kent are faint: an outline on a wall, a line in a will, largely unpublished and often hidden under their husband's name. They are hinted at in the architecture of a city, reminders, for example, of the Queen who enabled the cathedral, in its layout in relation to her own church.[1] Sometimes we see traces of the woman who enabled a book in the marginalia of the same, or in a footnote.

One such woman can be found, we think, **upon the wall of Rochester Cathedral**. There, on the east wall of the South Transept, can be found the faded remains of a wall-painting of two people either side of the blind arch, a man and a woman, facing each other, kneeling in prayer. It's often assumed that they are husband and wife, but there's no certainty. It is she who has her face turned to the onlooker, not the man kneeling opposite her. She is the one engaging the viewer in her vision of heaven. She is dressed in appropriately humble garb: a simple green frock, with her hair and neck covered by a wimple and veil. She kneels, hands outstretched in prayer, with an open book in front of her on a lectern.

Little can be seen now, but we have a painting, a copy, made a hundred years ago, that gives us a clue what it might once have looked like. It's hard to date paintings of this nature, but what we have (the dating of the creation of the blind arch and of the original Lady Chapel in the South Transept) puts this mural somewhere between 1240 and 1322, perhaps a little later but not much. During this time the cult of William of Perth[2] is just taking off. There's civil unrest during the 13th century (two civil wars, in fact), but the cathedral still manages to flourish on the back of the income from pilgrims. The time window for this mural closes just before the first wave of the Black Death hits Rochester in 1349.

Thanks to these earlier paintings by Professor EW Tristram, we know that the mural as a whole was decorated in little black, green and red roundels ornamented with red lions rampant. There was a traditional Annunciation scene: the Angel Gabriel, holding a scroll and gesturing towards the Virgin Mary. Either side of the arch, above our kneeling pair, were more angels. To the left of the painting, near the kneeling man, was Margaret of Antioch, dragon at her

---

[1] Go and stand in front of the door to St Martin's in Canterbury and see how it lines up with Queningate and the Cathedral.
[2] The source of much of the Cathedral's wealth during this period.

feet, lance in her hand. On the right of the picture, beyond the unnamed woman, was a picture of Catherine of Alexandria and her wheel. There was clearly once many more figures, at least one of them female, but these were already faded beyond recognition when the mural was copied in the 1920s. If the archway framed an altar, then our kneeling lady would have been looking at that altar, or perhaps at the presiding priest with the elevated sacrament, much like Joan Burghersh's tomb (we're coming to her). Both the kneeling figures were framed by painted vaulted arches. The whole construction was held together, visually, by vaults and pillars, as if to suggest a great extension to the Cathedral beyond the wall into the realm of heaven. There is not — and never was — anything remotely comparable to this down the road at Canterbury.[3]

That this apparently anonymous woman made it onto the wall of the cathedral is in fact extraordinary. Compare Rochester with her nearest relation, Canterbury, a cathedral of some size with *no contemporary women at all* on the walls. The only women painted on these walls are the ones playing necessary supporting roles in the story of a (male) saint, or are saints themselves. Not even in the crowd scenes are there any incidental women. Even the few women that there are — saints and the near relations of saints — are without exception the only woman in the scene. Nowhere are there two women together. Our Rochester lady on the other hand is *surrounded* by female saints. With the exception of possibly-but-not-necessarily-her-husband, the angel Gabriel plus choir, and some lions, it is a wall of women. On this wall of women, this wall of saints, it is our praying lady who gazes out of the picture, not her male partner. She is its centre, the creator of its energy. This is certainly unparalleled in Kent, and I suspect in England.

Now look at who has been chosen to surround her. Both Catherine and Margaret were two of the three principal saints among the Fourteen Holy Helpers, a group of saints considered to be particularly efficacious intercessors. Margaret was the woman's woman, a patron of women in childbirth (at the height

---

[3] #JustSaying

of her cult, she rivalled the Virgin Mary in popularity, and there were more churches named for her than for the mother of Jesus[4]). Catherine, tellingly, was the patron of, among other things, scholars and in particular female scholars (she died because she won an argument against 50 top-notch philosophers). Let me remind you at this point that our nameless wall lady is kneeling in front of an open book. Then add the fact that the third, and principal saint, Mary, is portrayed at the angel Gabriel's Annunciation to her. In mediaeval iconography, the Annunciation was consistently depicted with Mary beside an open book (steeping herself in the Word before becoming his home for nine months). Our kneeling lady has been drawn echoing the Virgin Mary, beside the patron saint of female scholars, with the patron of mothers, kneeling in prayer and/or study. Whoever our kneeling gentleman is, he's not the focus of this painting. This whole wall revolves around the woman in prayer.

The most likely explanation is that she is a patron, and a significant one, at that. There weren't many options open to a woman in the 13th century to get this kind of acclaim without leaving considerable evidence behind her. Even if she funded the mural herself, she must have built up some considerable credibility in the abbey for it to be permitted. Unfortunately comparatively little documentary evidence remains of Rochester Priory, so there is no certainty concerning the identity of this woman, but there is one important clue. Recent explorations of the mural at height, in a fashion unavailable to our Tristram a hundred years ago, have revealed more about her companion. The gentleman kneeling in prayer opposite our patroness sports what may be a gold leaf crown, and the suggestion of a red beard.

This is the point where we enter the realm of speculation, but not, mark you, of fantasy. See for yourself how the following lines up.

William II[5] was often known as William Rufus and it's usually assumed this was because of the colour of his

---

[4] including one just up the road from Rochester Cathedral
[5] The son of that William who showed up at Hastings with an army and a grudge concerning who Edward the Confessor may or may not have declared to be his heir.

hair. He is, in any case, often depicted with red hair. This William Rufus has left a couple of charters in the cathedral archives, both of which mention **Countess Goda**[6] as a significant benefactress, 'confirming'[7] Goda's gift of significant lands and of a book of the Gospels. She is, in fact, the only woman in the cathedral records to be mentioned making a gift entirely in her own name rather than coupled with her husband.

Countess Goda is the daughter of King Ethelred and of Emma of Normandy. (Emma is a woman who, herself, had a reputation for intelligence and education, increasing the likelihood of Goda's being likewise educated.) This parentage makes Goda the niece to King Edmund the martyr (feast day: 20 November) and to Edith of Kemsing (who we'll come to later) and sister to Edward the Confessor (feast day: 13 October). We know that the commemoration of her as a donor took place annually with literal bells and figurative whistles. The lands she gave provided the cathedral with a significant income, but perhaps of more interest to us in relation to this mural is the book that she gave which bears her name.

At the time of the construction of the Lady Chapel and the design of the mural, the Cathedral's library and records were being rebuilt after they had been trashed repeatedly during the 13th century by war and fire. One of the library's most valuable manuscripts, *Customale Roffense*, was added during this time, as well as a number of key commentaries and collections. Moreover, we have the beginning of some serious scholarship among the monks of Rochester from the late 1320s, with the first monks being sent to Oxford to study. We know that a significant drive for the scholarly culture of the Priory was to establish their pre-conquest credibility and legitimacy, underlining the Priory's links to the early Christian kings of Kent, Mercia and Wessex.

---

[6] a.k.a. – you guessed it – Godgifu, Godgyfu, and Godiva (no, not the naked horseback lady, although they were near contemporaries).
[7] it was not unheard of for legacies at this time to take a couple of "detours" on their way to their destination, whilst still being considered a gift of the original owner. Goda's property clearly spent a period of half a century or so benefiting the new Royal Family, before landing where she had intended it.

I have pointed out, have I not, Goda's royal, and indeed saintly, bloodline?

Goda's book of the Gospels was originally in a bejewelled cover and it seems likely that the text influenced subsequent gospel manuscripts at Rochester, having as it does a number of distinctive readings. Her book was important enough to the Cathedral Priory that early in its history some anonymous scribe added her name to it ("*belongs to Church at Rochester, through Countess Goda*"). It's one of only four books listed in the Rochester collection as a '*textus*', one of only two to survive to this day. Like the other surviving *textus* (Roffensis) this is described as *textus de ecclesiae* (Church) rather than the more usual *textus de claustro* (cloister). *Textus* sets it apart as a precious text; *de ecclesiae* suggests that it was kept, not in the library or the scriptorium, but in the church proper, in a place of honour. On the altar of the Lady Chapel, perhaps, in line with the pictorial gaze of the lady who gave it?

If the possibly crowned, possibly redheaded, figure opposite Probably-Goda is William Rufus, the one who restored her donation; the son of the Duke of Normandy in whose hospitality Goda's son[8] met a sudden and unexpected end, the probability of it being Goda is stronger still.

In truth, we do not know for sure who this lady was, although Goda is a good candidate. That such a woman, who made enough of an impact on the cathedral to have a *wall* dedicated to her, has left scant trace in the written record demonstrates the invisibility of so many of these women in history. Even Goda we know very little about despite her wealth, probable learning and her aristocracy, despite even her considerable responsibilities as a landowner.[9] Women up and down Kent were supporting artists, scholars, priests, monks and nuns in the service of God. We just don't have their names.

---

[8] A favourite of Edward the Confessor, and, who knows, possible rival to the throne. Is there some blood-guilt on William's conscience?
[9] Of further weight to her identification with the Wall Lady, is the fact that she founded a church on her estates in London (part of her legacy to the Cathedral) which was dedicated to Mary, who is beside her on the wall.

One woman who made sure her name was remembered, wrote it in stone. She is not quite a contemporary of our Rochester mural, being born about twenty years after the latest date of the mural's completion. **Joan Burghersh**'s[10] birth is not recorded, but it is likely to be around 1341. She is born of a Kentish family (the Burgheshes) and marries a distant cousin, Sir John De Mohun of Dunster. The first of only three women to be buried in Canterbury Cathedral, her tomb is extraordinary. Her alabaster image is not quite under Thomas Becket's shrine, and just about inside the Undercroft Chapel she helped fund. Eternally liminal, her slightly off-centre location gives her effigy sight of the statue of the Virgin as well as a probable sight-line for the elevated host at that altar (like Probably-Goda). Her hands (when she had them) were folded in prayer.

Burghersh's married life does not seem to have been terribly happy. There is a legend that she walked barefoot around a chunk of ground in Dunster in order to persuade her husband to give it as common land, but it seems likely that this is just a re-churning of the Lady Godiva myth. There is no evidence of any such transaction during her husband's tenure. Her husband's death, however, liberates her to use both her connections and her resources to considerable advantage. Both Burghersh's brother and her husband are original members of the Order of the Garter, being friends of the Black Prince. On Sir John's death, Burghersh and her daughter Elizabeth are permitted to wear livery of the Order of the Garter. Ladies of the Garter took part in the Order's ceremonies and celebrations. They swore ornate oaths tying them to the objectives of knights at war. They were not to ask their male relatives to return from war, they were to help male relatives if they were besieged and they were even to use their own dowry (but only up to half) if it was needed for a ransom.

Sir John dies in 1375 (a year before the Black Prince) and is buried in Somerset with his family, but Burghersh does not retire into widowly grief. She remains at Court, clearly influential. She is given

---

[10] Also known as the Lady of Dunster, Joan (Lady) de Mohun, Joan Burwaschs, Joan Burwash, Joan de Burghersh, Joan de Moune and Johane de Borwasche. Naturally.

Leeds Castle, near Maidstone, apparently in part payment for her services as an estate agent to the Court. Burghersh is further woven into Court connections when she fosters one of John of Gaunt's daughters. Her own daughters all marry extremely well, which is perhaps just as well because she sells her husband's family estate, effectively dis-inheriting them. Burghersh then goes on to give nearly £34 (which you can times by nearly a thousand for a modern equivalent) for the furnishing of the new chapel in the crypt of Canterbury Cathedral: The Undercroft.[11] The chapel itself is remarkable, and we can assume Burghersh has had a say in its design. It was usual for the patron to choose the artisans and designers and therefore to have a considerable influence over the final product. This chapel, then, speaks of Burghersh's religion.

Rather than the usual blue for a Lady Chapel, it has a red ceiling and reredos, which would have made the chapel womb-like, or heart-like — either way, deeply, organically female. In the ceiling she has set gaudy glass beads and mirror discs to bring eternity and the arc of heaven into the underground chapel. Like Burghersh's tomb, the chapel is broadly liminal, boundary crossing. The womb is par excellence a world between worlds, and placing the stars of heaven underground creates a sense of here-but-there, splicing two worlds together. This is by a woman who is a member of a Knights' order, who alienated her own family, who existed at the fringes of power. For all her influence, did Burghersh never quite fit in?

It is presumably this patronage that buys Burghersh her unique place in the cathedral. The chantry deed is written in 1395 and the tomb completed in 1399. Burghersh spends the last years of her life as a prestigious guest of the prior, in the cathedral guesthouse of Meister Omers. The chantry deed leaves 350 marks a piece to the monks of the abbey, which was a lot. It also includes vestments, linen, a missal, a chalice and, oddly, a bed and bedding. It also stipulates that as well as the Requiem to be said

---

[11] (By a curious coincidence, Burghersh liquidates the necessary funds from her husband's estate to finance the chapel in the same year that the Black Prince dies and permission is granted for laypeople to be buried in the cathedral. Correlation, if not causation.)

on the anniversary of her death, money should be given to the poor. Her chantry priests are to be dressed in vestments made from her own bed-hangings (which, as they were embroidered with Burghersh's crest, puts that nicely on display). The monks are to say masses for nine people: for Burghersh herself, four royal connections and four members of her family (but only one of her daughters.[12]) In her will, written five years later, two days before she died, we find a range of domestic and ecclesiastical bequests as well as her funeral arrangements and a bequest setting up three scholarships.

On the face of it, Burghersh might be considered the opposite of our Rochester patron. Far from the latter's humble attire, Burghersh is dressed in death in fashionable court attire and hairstyle, her name set in stone, displaying the evidence of her patronage and her patrons. She wears huge buttons with the Regent John of Gaunt's crest displayed (which is also the crest of the Black Prince). Although the crest of the Order in the chapel where she is interred may not have been added by her, both those crests and the Black Prince's own tomb tie her into a network of affiliation with royal authority and religious devotion, in death as she was in life.

We can't see into her heart, and there is less evidence of her everyday life than there is even for Eleanor Plantagenet or Anne Boleyn. Church and Court and power and devotion are all woven together in her bequests and in her tomb. Like the painting of Probably-Goda, that tomb lays Burghersh out for eternity with the eyes of her effigy fixed on the celebration of the mass (while reminding you who her friends were). As with Goda, the impact of the money that she gave to the cathedral must have been significant. The chapel that she helped pay for lasts to this day as an oasis in a world at least as complicated as hers.

---

[12] Of the two not included, one daughter was already dead and there are traces that the other never forgave her mother for disinheriting her. She was, by marriage, the Duchess of York and Burghersh left in her will simply "her blessing," and - its not clear - either a bottle of wine or a ruby. Perhaps Burghersh was hoping her alienated daughter would toast her memory.

Somewhere between these two, the most gaudy and the most discrete of patrons we find **Charlotte Boyd**. Boyd is born in 1837, a child of the Empire, born in Macau. The day she's born, 21st of March, in the calendar of saints of the time is feast day of St Benedict, a fact that seems to accompany her by way of an omen or fate. Before she is a year old her family moves back to Blighty and she spends her childhood in Brighton, an Anglo-Catholic hub. Indeed, when the young Boyd is just 18 one of the very early sisterhoods is founded in Brighton, which makes an impact on a teenage imagination already imbued with the romance of monasticism. According to her own account, when she is just 13 she visits Glastonbury Abbey and kneels in the ruins to offer herself to the "work of restoration."

As has already been mentioned, the Victorian woman was expected to devote herself to her family and her home. Intrinsic, therefore, to Boyd's ability to commit herself to this teenage vision is the death of almost her entire family over an eight-year period during the 1860s. Her one remaining brother is apparently content to let her crack on with her own projects. This somewhat brutal de-familiarisation not only liberates her time and attention, but also gives her the resources that she needs, as she inherits from one relation after another. Intrinsic, too, is the fact that Boyd remains single all her life, despite one or two persistent courtships (she was said to have a "pleasant countenance," and to be "good looking were it not for very bad teeth"). Her biographer, Yelton, speculates, reasonably, that had she been induced to marry, very little of the work she accomplished would have been undertaken.

After consulting with the founder of her local house, the Rev Dr JM Neale, she starts her own project in Kensington.

Victorian urban life, as we've established, was filthy, brutal, with a social safety net that was more holes than net. The life expectancy was 40, but when you account for all of the urban Victorians that made it into their old age, this means a lot of them were dying in their 20s. The result was an awful lot of unaccompanied minors — and Victorian London was a nasty place to be an unaccompanied minor. Boyd's philanthropic drive, therefore, leads her in 1866 to set up a small orphanage for girls in Kensington. This establishment grows and as it grows it needs to move again and again into more suitable accommodation. As her orphanage develops, Boyd remains in touch with the local clergy, in particular with the Revd RC Kirkpatrick, with whom there seems to be some sort of slow burn romance.

Then, in 1875, Boyd sets up the English Abbey Restoration Trust, which is rich in members but poor in funds. Its purpose was to purchase former ecclesiastical buildings that had fallen into secular ownership, particularly during the Reformation. In 1883, she responds to an advert posted in the magazine *Our Work*[13] by Bella Blunt — a member of the family that owns Malling Abbey — and she rents the gatehouse and Pilgrim Chapel at Malling Abbey. (Boyd has had her eye on the Abbey from the beginning of the trust, but the owners would not sell. They were, nonetheless, devout Tractarians who had been lending the gatehouse to a London sisterhood. These sisters, of the Community of St Peter, had initially wanted a retirement home but had segued into using the place to train young girls for domestic service. When they left, the family looked for a more permanent arrangement and advertised accordingly.)

Boyd offers the Abbey gatehouse to the sisters from the newly founded Community of the Holy Comforter. (It is this Community of the Holy Comforter that seeds the current community at Malling, after Mtr Hilda's community submits to Rome.) There, Boyd continues and extends her work with orphans. At the same sort of time, Boyd encounters Hilda and the sisters of SS Mary and Scholastica. She begins to assist them financially, particularly after their lease of the Feltham farmhouse comes to an end in 1889. She becomes an oblate of the community, but never takes vows.

---

[13] a rag run by the Sisters of the Church, Kilburn. As it happens Isabella Gilmore was at this time newly widowed and training in nursing. In her later memoirs she writes scathingly about people who "with the best intentions do harm" because they "had in no sense felt themselves servants of the clergy and the church but it was '*Our Work*' & if ever individuals or Communities get that idea into their hearts the work for God must suffer loss." (my emphasis) it may just be me, but this looks like a dig.

During this time two sisterhoods close to Boyd in London make moves to encourage her to commit to the religious life, the better to conduct the work of philanthropy. One is a nursing sisterhood, outside Boyd's specialism, but the other is a large organisation running youth and children's work, in education and orphanages, altogether caring for over 600 children. It is this community, the Sisters of the Church, whose magazine Boyd subscribes to, but she never signs up for the religious life. Had she done so, just as if she had married, she would have lost control of her assets and ceased to be the philanthropist she was just becoming.

In 1891 Boyd's remaining uncle shuffles off this mortal coil leaving behind a considerable fortune for his niece — almost a million in today's money. Finally having her hands on substantial funds means that Boyd can again bid for the Malling property. This time circumstances favour her. The widow in residence has died and her heir is anxious to sell.[14] Boyd's inheritance means that she is able to bid high — had history taken a different turn, and her competitors for the property succeeded, the Abbey would have instead become a teahouse! Boyd has been waiting, by her own reckoning, nearly 40 years for this opportunity and she is not going to let it pass.

The purchase is advertised by the English Abbey Restoration Trust and has in its terms that any community in occupation must be in Communion with Canterbury. This is to become significant in the history of the Abbey. Something seems to be going on in the background of the English Abbey Restoration Trust at the time because Boyd doesn't use it to buy Malling Abbey, and she also resigns as treasurer. Nevertheless, the Trust cheerfully anticipates in its newsletter that "once again the divine office so long silenced will be recited day by day and the one sacrifice be daily pleaded." Their hopes are fulfilled when the sisters of St Mary and St Scholastica move in during Easter week, 1893. It is Boyd's expressed wish that the community should pray for Christian unity. Although the wording she chose (saying a daily

---

[14] there is an agricultural depression at the time

mass "for the union of the Churches"[15]) was rejected, the final wording, praying for "the will of God" is nevertheless intended to convey the same thing. The community at Malling continues in that commitment to this day.

Buoyed by her success, so to speak, Boyd turns her sights to Walsingham. Her intention is to buy that Priory also, but again she's thwarted by the owners' refusal to sell. Instead she buys the Slipper Chapel, then being used as a barn on the outskirts of the property. Negotiations must have begun almost as soon as the nuns were installed at Malling Abbey, but the purchase does not go through until 26 June 1896. As an Anglican, it is tempting to speculate on the 'if only' of a somewhat swifter purchase, which would have left the Slipper Chapel either in the hands of the English Abbey Restoration Trust, or in the subsidiary trust created for Malling Abbey — and therefore dedicated to remain in communion with Canterbury. As it is, in September 1894 Boyd submits to Rome, and so the Slipper Chapel instead passes into the heritage of the Roman Catholic Church in this country.

Boyd never seems to have expressed any doubts about her conversion, even though at the time Rome was much less enthusiastic about the restoration project than the Church of England (a low bar to fail to clear). The Slipper Chapel is not developed into a shrine until 1934, nearly 30 years after Boyd's death. Boyd's conversion is preceded by pilgrimage to the shrine of Our Lady in Belgium, followed by a retreat in the English convent at Bruges. It may be that her failing health encourages her to commit wholly to a tradition that already has its religious houses and retreat centres established.

After Boyd's conversion, the expectation on both sides is that she should empty her orphanages of all Anglicans and staff it with Roman Catholics for Roman Catholics. In our current age of ecumenism, it's hard to imagine the levels of acrimony that existed between the denominations. The rivalry for souls was acrimonious in the extreme, and those who changed their allegiance were labelled as traitors. Only full and

---

[15] The phrase looked, to Anglican Victorian ears, a little too close to seeking unification with Rome – heaven forfend.

complete immersion could mitigate the distrust. Boyd refuses, even though the current staff, bitter and angered by her change of denomination, attempt to have her removed from the charity and replaced with an Anglican. Despite Westminster appointing May Quinlan as the secretary of the institution, Boyd insists on allowing the Anglicans to be replaced organically, as they leave in their own time. She even manages to maintain friendly relations with the Church of England parish in which the orphanage sits (remember Kirkpatrick?).

Our patron's health continues to collapse. Her diabetes, then untreatable, leads inexorably to blindness, kidney failure and at length death on 3 April 1906, aged 68. Her considerable wealth has all been spent on her concern for the poor and on her commitment to seeing the religious life restored in England. Her family refuses to bury her in the family vault, on account of her conversion; the Roman Church, having never quite trusted her because she failed to break all her links with the Church of England, also refuses to bury her with honour. She's buried, therefore, in an unmarked grave in St Mary's Roman Catholic Cemetery in Kensal Green. Without Boyd's input, her orphanage dwindles and closes. The Slipper Chapel remains mothballed and the sisters of SS Mary and Scholastica soon leave Malling Abbey and, shortly after, themselves convert to Rome. Boyd is almost completely forgotten. Both the Church of England and the Church of Rome labelled her a traitor because of her love for the other, so neither celebrate her. Her grave is not even marked as hers until 1962, when she is finally, and, it seems, slightly grudgingly, given the iron cross that a religious oblate warrants.

Her legacy is huge. In her lifetime she spent all she had on the Church and her poor. If you measure her life only in terms of the orphans that she rescued from destitution, it is significant enough. Her contribution to spiritual life in this country, however, cannot be measured. Today, about a quarter of a million people make the pilgrimage to Walsingham each year. The Abbey at West Malling continues a life of prayer at the heart of the Anglican Diocese of Rochester. Moreover, the site not only supports a retreat and conference centre but a theological college that trains both ordinands and laity for ministry. In 1982 she finally got a memorial: the headstone and cross on her grave were transferred to Walsingham, outside the Slipper Chapel that she rescued. (Her grave was marked instead with a simple plaque.) There is nothing to commemorate her in Kent: only the sisters at Malling Abbey faithfully remember Boyd every year on 3 April, and in their prayers for the faithful departed.

None of the women in this chapter rank high on the priority of historians. They are often the very definition of 'well behaved women,' embedded in their domestic lives, caring for kith and kin (well, maybe not Burghersh) and supporting the religious fabric of the Church around them. They were business women, shrewd financiers, organised and often artistic, enabling the work of others. Through the centuries, their contribution has been both assumed and relied upon. Their likeness is modelled in almost every parish church, in the women who clean the church and mend the linen, who pay faithfully, perhaps sacrificially, into the parish coffers, and who step up time and time again, quietly and steadfastly, to do, and to give, what is necessary.

It begs the question why we do not, as a Church, celebrate these people more. I suspect the answer is that, just like power, the Church of England is deeply uncomfortable talking about money. It smacks of Mammon, of idolatry, and is laced with English middle-class distaste. However, failing to celebrate these women sells short theirs and other's contributions, often made at great sacrifice, made for the glory of God. It sends an unspoken message parallel to every stewardship campaign: 'we want your money, but we won't value you for giving it to us.' For all the Church declares that giving is an important part of discipleship, the calendar of saints is adamant that it is not any kind of demonstration of holiness.

Peacemakers and power-brokers

"Blessed are the peacemakers, for they will be called children of God."

The role of women across the centuries has often been behind the scenes, by virtue of the constraints on their ability to exercise power. This very background position, along with the social training in networking and negotiation which comes from limited power, often places women in an ideal position to broker and negotiate power. Not wielding it, but they become its fulcrum, the point on which it turns; never holding it, they affect where it lies and how it's exercised.

At the turn of the century the United Nations passed a resolution enshrining the role of women in peacemaking. When women are signatories in peace agreements, says the UN, there is a statistically verifiable correlation in the durability of the resulting peace. In part, this is simply down to the fact that if a woman has fought hard enough to get to the table, she will have more determination to see it through, but there is more to it than that. There are gender specific interests — that domesticity again, as well as a general disinclination to be raped or otherwise abused: women often have the most to lose when violence erupts.

This chapter, then, looks at the peacemakers and powerbrokers, women who have changed the lie of the land by pulling strings and being in the right place at the right time. These women are often undersold because they are not the principal actors in the drama, but they are the ones that make the action possible.

Take **Pocahontas**. Pocahontas has a tendency to be a Rorschach test[16] for the person commentating on her. She has been a figurehead for both the North and the South during the American Civil War. She is a

---

[16] That thing where you look at ink blots and what you see Reveals All.

feminist; she is The Good Wife. She is the undiscovered land of America, The Good Indian,[17] but she is also the heroine of the Native American. She is a romantic heroine — though, disturbingly, the romance is usually attributed to John Smith, who only knew her as a child.[18] She is, in short, all things to all people. Much of this is because she doesn't tell her own tale; the telling of her story, from the start, is propaganda by an alien culture.

We *know* very little. Her date of birth is unclear, but is towards the very end of the 16th century in what is now Virginia. She is born Mataoka, but we will continue to call her by her nickname, Pocahontas, because that's the name by which she is generally known. Her people describe themselves as the Tsenacommacah, and it's a semi-settled agricultural society. Pocahontas' father is Powhatan, a local leader not only of his own community but of some sort of federation of settlements. Pocahontas is one of 20 siblings and not — despite European assumptions — politically significant by birth. (The English settlers at the time assume equivalence with monarchy, so they describe Pocahontas in royal terms, but we now know the comparison doesn't stand. The leadership of the Tsenacommacah was matrilineal, so it was Powhatan's brothers, not his children who succeeded him.) Nevertheless Powhatan is a local leader of some considerable influence who clearly trusts his daughter: she is sufficiently respected by her father to run a trade and prisoner exchange programme with Jamestown.

It is on such a trading exercise that Pocahontas meets John Smith when the latter arrives in Virginia in 1608. In his first account, written at the time, he says she's about 10 years old, but he later amends this to 13. In his description of her she is clearly intelligent, engaging and empathetic. The food she and the other children bring that day saves the colony from starvation, recounts Smith. She is also bold and joyful, coming into the town in a small crowd of children, mostly boys, naked as the day she was born, turning cartwheels. She is generally charming, but the heroism Disney attributes to her is less certain. It is

---

[17] don't @ me – there's no good way of saying it
[18] Looking at you, Disney.

possible over the course of the next year that there was some sort of fraught encounter between John Smith and Pocahontas' people, but it's really not very clear and may be fiction. I'll come back to this. In 1609 Smith leaves Jamestown with severe burns on account of an accident, and Pocahontas, for some reason, is told that he is dead.

There is a single account that Pocahontas then marries one of her own people, a chap of some standing, allegedly, called Kocoum, but if this did take place there seems to be a common agreement by all concerned to forget about it afterwards. Certainly nobody takes any existing marriage into account when in 1613 Pocahontas is kidnapped.

She is staying in a neighbouring territory, Patawomech, when Capt Samuel Argall persuades some of the local people — whom our heroine presumably trusted — to encourage her to join them on a tour of the British ship, *The Treasurer,* anchored on the River Potomac. Out of some vestige of civilised behaviour Argall does at least feed his guests before locking Pocahontas in the gunner's room. By all accounts she doesn't take this well. By some accounts she is not treated well.

The prisoner is taken back to Jamestown and her father contacted in the hope of a prisoner exchange. Powhatan is content to return the prisoners with the sweetener of food that the settlers ask for but he refuses to send back the weapons that had been captured with the Englishmen. Pocahontas therefore remains in Jamestown, and the people there set about converting her to the True Faith. She is baptised later that year, becoming Rebecca, and in 1614 marries John Rolfe with whom she has a son, Thomas, the following year. According to some accounts it is on Pocahontas' account that John's tobacco farming succeeds as well as it does and his trade in the carcinogenic leaf flourishes.

In 1616 she accompanies John Rolfe back to England and is fêted much like Sarah Bonetta will be. She is called the 'Indian princess' and 'Lady Rebecca'. Not long after, in 1617, she meets John Smith again, having believed him dead for eight years. She is understandably disgruntled and he records her words of rebuke, even though it seems he doesn't understand them. After this she and Rolfe prepare to return to Virginia, but within days she sickens and dies in Gravesend, where she's buried. John Rolfe purportedly mourns her loss — and uses her image to sell his tobacco.

Before long Powhatan also dies and is succeeded by his half-brother who leads a catastrophic attack on the people of Jamestown. It's catastrophic for both sides: the people of Jamestown are decimated, but it also spells the end of any attempt towards peaceful relations between the two communities. With not a little irony, Rolfe dies in the conflict, and relationships such as his with Pocahontas are soon after made illegal. It is after this massacre, in 1624, that John Smith's account of his near death experience at Powhatan's hands is publicised.

Pocahontas' story is riddled with ambiguity. Even the name by which she is commonly known, now commonly interpreted as 'little mischief' was understood by the settlers to mean 'little wanton'. (They were considerably shocked by her nakedness as a child, and by the general lack of corsets in the adult women, leading them to assume, of course, that all the women were promiscuous.) The name she took on baptism was allegedly a reference to Isaac's wife, who bore two sons, one — so the European interpretation ran — pale, and one *red skinned*. Her name was intended to convey her ability to engage with both cultures, although everything about her trip to London was intended to imply the triumph of European civilisation over her barbaric origins.

There are a lot of parallels to be drawn with Sarah Forbes Bonetta. Both women were kidnapped from their familial context, both thoroughly Europeanised, both fêted by the English Court as foreign royalty (but foreign royalty who had been brought to heel, culturally and spiritually). Like Bonetta she was set up and funded to run a mission among her own people (somewhat aborted by her death). There is one piece of evidence, however, which suggests Pocahontas had considerably more agency than her African sister: the strip that John Smith records being removed from his hide, care of Pocahontas' tongue lashing. "You did promise Powhatan what was yours should be his, and he the like to you," she says. She makes a clear case of kinship, which she thinks he has reneged on.

This brings us to the Strange Incident with the Rock. In his later account, John Smith describes an incident in which the tone of an encounter with Powhatan suddenly changes. He says two large stones were brought out and his head was forcibly laid on the one and the community looks set to murder him with the other. Pocahontas then runs forward and lays her head over his, so that they cannot kill him without killing her. The nascent stoning is aborted and instead John Smith is clasped to the community bosom.

Even at the time, this episode lacked credibility because it wasn't included in his original account, and to this day remains contentious. It is not uncommented on that Smith doesn't tell his story until both the other principal witnesses are dead. It is also pointed out that his narrative helps to equip the hardened attitude against the people of the Tsenacommacah, portraying Pocahontas, as it does, as the exception to a brutal and barbaric culture. It is this event, nevertheless, that tends to take pride point in romantic accounts of Pocahontas. Since the 60s, however, there has developed a theory that this may well be a true account, which perhaps Smith was sheepish to record at the time because it shows him helpless in the hands of the Other, and rescued by a Girl. However, the theory goes, although the account is a genuine recollection it is not a faithful record: Smith fundamentally misunderstood what was going on.

There are apparently sufficient parallels in Native American culture to indicate that what Smith was experiencing was an adoption ritual and that the whole thing was staged. What Smith thought was a genuine attempt to kill him was potentially ritual death, followed by rescue by Powhatan's kin. By ritually stepping into the breach, Pocahontas was taking responsibility for Smith's life and becoming his bridge to the Tsenacommacah community. This casts a different light on her father's refusing to ransom her, leaving her in the European Community, especially when she travels to Europe accompanied by a Tsenacommacah holy man who is evidently briefed to do a recce. This sits better in accord with the opening picture we have of her as trusted and confident, equipped to conduct missions among the settlers. This is not a romance, it's a diplomatic mission. Her death, in this light, could have precipitated a breakdown in relations between the two communities because the go-between was lost. Where the English thought they had a compliant female of royal line, the Tsenacommacah thought they had an inside woman, a diplomat — a spy, even. When she dies, they turn instead (disastrously) to direct action.

It is quite feasible that Pocahontas takes advantage of her situation to build bridges. She has been kidnapped — possibly even raped — but she's been a negotiator and trader from her childhood. It's possible, of course, that she was abandoned by her own people and in a sort of Stockholm Syndrome-esque reaction adopted the culture of her kidnappers. It is also possible that she decided to take advantage — possibly in collaboration with her father — of a grim situation. Remember the presence of her own people's holy men with her on the trip to Europe? It speaks against all ties with her roots being cut.

Her marriage is then, in a sense, the reverse operation of mission-by-marriage. Instead of showing up with her own culture and support team, like the Kentish Princesses, she immerses herself in the Other. She steps into the mores and spirituality of the stranger in order better to understand and negotiate. Even today she is by way of an entry point to Native American culture — for good or for ill — to the point where she is probably the only Native American, fictional or historic, that most Europeans can name, often being the Face of Thanksgiving in American homes. She is perhaps as much as 20 when she dies. Who knows what she would have achieved if she'd be able to return to Virginia with the insights that she had gained from a visit to the colonisers' home? If that mission, funded during her trip to London, had taken place, could the European colonisation of America involved more integration and less slaughter? There is, alas, no parallel universe available to us to know.

There is, however, another negotiator-queen, who does make it to old age, does make a long-term difference. About a thousand years earlier, **Domne**

Eafe[19] is working for fair restitution, while avoiding escalation. Domne Eafe is Queen Bertha's great-granddaughter. It is possible that she is another missionary in the mission-by-marriage with the continuing-to-practice-her-religion and the clerical-support-group add-on. Her husband, Merewalh of Mercia converts to Christianity somewhere around 660 A.D. which could well have been around the time of his marriage. When Merewalh dies, Domne Eafe returns to Kent to discover that her brothers have been murdered. Here's where we step firmly into the 'some say' brand of storytelling.

Some say that Eadbald's younger son, Eorcenberht (Bertha's grandson), became King not by merit but by trickery. (Inheritance in Anglo-Saxon England, as far as we can tell, was not straightforward primogeniture.) He takes his big brother's sons into his own household, in a gesture that is variously placed on a scale of dastardly cunning through fraternal affection, depending on the storyteller. The boys are educated under his roof and are well liked but not ambitious (theirs was a "voluntary neglect of secular advantages"). Eorcenberht is succeeded by his own son, Ecgberht, in or around 664 A.D. The nephews/cousins are now embarrassing, in a Princes-in-the-Tower kind of way.

Enter Thunor, Ecgberht's right hand man; cue ominous thunder. He is cast in the role of Iago and shadow to the brothers' shining sun of saintliness. The story goes that he loathes the two princes and, with a varying amount of complicity on Ecgberht's part, again depending on who's telling the story, Thunor murders the princes. Heaven only knows why, but he decides it's a good idea to bury the two corpses under the King's throne. Shockingly, the bodies are discovered, but not because somebody looks at the freshly turned earth under the King's throne and thinks, that's odd. Rather, it's because, on the princes being missed, a shining light from heaven is cast ("at midnight, through the roof of the hall, as if the sun were shining there,") upon the spot where the corpses are hidden. Thunor is now in the frame and throws his boss, Ecgberht, under the proverbial bus.

---

[19] a.k.a. Domneva, Domne Éue, Æbbe, Ebba and possibly Eormenburg, Imenburg and Ermenburga. Go figure.

In a rather fun parenthesis of the story, the corpses proceed to refuse burial at either of the competing houses in Canterbury (we will get to this story, when we discuss Mildthryth) then consent to be buried locally, in a religious house that Domne Eafe's youngest daughter eventually settles in, in nearby Wenlock.

Here's where Domne Eafe comes in. However the story is told, by now you have the potential for a serious blood feud. This is the stuff of which wars are made. Two very well-connected young men have been killed. Domne Eafe is not only related to the local royal line, but also has powerful allies in Mercia. The story splits into two tracks. In one version Ecgberht is penitent and simply offers her a parcel of land and the foundation of an abbey by way of compensation. It's an impressive display of his attempts to make amends. In the other, Domne Eafe negotiates and gets the expanse of land that her hind can run about in a day. Now, the hind turns out to be surprisingly athletic and persistent either (yet again, depending on the teller) because God is directing the deer or because Domne Eafe is so holy that the deer is guided and strengthened by her. Either way, the hind circles an impressively large stretch of land.

Rather wonderfully, Thunor is said to be so outraged by the impressive wergild[20] that he tries to catch the deer, fails a jump that the hind cleared and drowns in a watercourse now called — or at the time of the telling was called, in any case — Thunor's Leap.

This is a story of conflict averted. Domne Eafe in effect neutralises her own blood claims and takes herself and the wergild into the Church (itself troubling to later chroniclers because the Church was not supposed to receive blood money). She takes a situation that could easily have led to war and instead creates a religious foundation that dominates the economy and culture of East Kent for a couple of hundred years. In the years to come, this house would receive impressive tax exemptions and its abbesses would be the witnesses on a succession of charters. Domne Eafe's daughter, Mildthryth, becomes the

---

[20] Lit. "human gold" – blood price – cf glossary

surety of holiness for several communities who will, literally, squabble for her bones.

There is an interpretation of this legend that argues that it was descriptive of the throwing down of the Kentish gods in favour of the Christian[21]. Even if this is so, it still argues for a memory of Domne Eafe negotiating the cultural grief in such a way as to leave significant capital (geographical as well as social) in the hands of the Church. Given the number of martyrs in most of the countries that Christianity enters, and the lack of them in Kent, this itself is no mean feat.

Even under all of the myth and legend of the story surrounding her, her name says it all. The name by which she is most commonly known, Domne Eafe/Domnever, probably means The Abbess/Lady Abbess. When you remember all that we have considered regarding the significance of the abbesses in this period, their connections and their influence, this is some accolade. *The Abbess* was a power-broker, a negotiator, who brought peace to the area and credibility — as well as serious resources — to the mission of the Church.

Even after the women's houses were significantly reduced in their autonomy in the 10th and 11th centuries, we see the mediaeval convents still taking a similar role. In a corner plot just beyond the urban fringe of Canterbury, within St Augustine's shadow, four nuns set up **the community of Holy Sepulchre** (which would become the home, much later, of Elizabeth Barton). It is registered in the Domesday book records as four acres of land from St Augustine's, held by the nuns. Not long after, at the turn of the 11th century, Anselm regularised the community, making the community a corner plot, ecclesiastically as well as geographically. The land was owned by one ecclesiastical power, the foundation governed by another. To add to the liminality between town and church, between the archepiscopal see and one of the city's principal monasteries, a co-founder with Anselm was the city's portreeve, William de Cauvel, a sort of Mayor-come-Police-Commissioner. The nunnery sat at the centre of a Venn diagram of spheres of influence.

---

[21] "Thunor" being suspiciously similar to "Thor".

The corner plot they held was in itself significant. It sat on the boundary between St Augustine's land and the liberty of the city of Canterbury. Moreover the Dover Road along which it was placed was one of the King's Roads, and within the King's jurisdiction, policed though it was by the city authorities. Also in the shadow of the nunnery was the Beast Market, which may well be the market that Cauvel moved, in the teeth of the Archbishop's wishes, causing some Church/state tension. Neither here nor there, the convent sat on all the principal boundaries of geography and power, with a finger in pretty much every pie.

The community was hardly invisible in terms of property, either, and where there is property there is both influence and power — even when the sisters' movements were restricted. They owned the local parish church, assorted land within the city and a steady trickle of gifts, land and rents. The control of a graveyard gave them still more leverage. The early adoption of a seal for the nunnery suggests a significant impact on the bureaucracy of the city.

You can see, in the paper trail that the community left behind, a record of powers played one against the other: of the nuns forbidden from certain corners of the city belonging to St Augustine's Abbey, of the convent buying up Jewish property during the heyday of anti-Semitism in the 13th century (intriguingly, they continue to record it as belonging to its original Jewish owner), of the prioresses' activity in the courts and successive archbishops constraining and then re-constraining their actions. The Archbishop's visitations not only record contention regarding the proper behaviour of the nuns, they also record the prioresses deploying the Archbishop into their own grievances: rents not paid, the noise of the Beast Market disturbing their midnight devotions. The steady trickle of clerics sponsored through holy orders by the nunnery likewise extended the tendrils of their influence.

The convent was never big. The greatest extent of their size seems to have been 12 nuns, and by the 16th century they were down to five. It was suppressed in the first wave of dissolutions mopping up all the small institutions. They had little power of their own, but they knew how to deploy the carefully balanced civic and ecclesiastical powers around them. By a process of exchange, negotiation and reciprocity, the little nunnery had an impact well beyond its wealth or size. They protected their own interests, but also those of other minorities. They were a source of vocations and were patrons in their own right. They were a place where lines of power met and were negotiated.

An abbess whose skill at this is largely overlooked is born at the point that the shape of the religious life of women is shifting. King Edgar's second wife (although there is an element of inverted commas around 'wife'), **Wulfthryth**, is born towards the end of the 930s. The principal source for our knowledge of Wulfthryth's life is told by Goscelin, he who is so sceptical about Eadburh's identity. This time, however, he is writing within living memory and almost certainly spoke to nuns who had known Wulfthryth. It's also likely, however, that he might have polished up the story, just a tad. Beyond his account, the stories speak less well of the libidinous King (who doesn't come out at well even in Goscelin's version).

The story goes that Edgar, his first wife having died, probably in childbirth, casts around for a solid alliance for wife number two. His eyes settle on Wulfhild, Wulfthryth's cousin. She, everyone has agreed, is a fully signed up veiled and vowed nun and is, as the film[22] has it, disinclined to acquiesce to his request. Edgar is not a man to take no for an answer and pursues his intended to her aunt's house. This aunt appears to have established one of the more informal religious setups mentioned in chapter 1, because Wulfhild is extremely surprised when Edgar shows up for dinner. Wulfhild legs it once again, this time to the more formal establishment of Wilton. However, we know that small things like religious vows do not have an enormous impact on Edgar.[23] During the monastic reforms that take place during his reign, while Edgar is put in charge of all the monasteries, the ecclesiastics of the time do not trust him with the

---

[22] *Pirates of the Caribbean, Walt Disney Pictures (2003)*
[23] His habit of seducing/raping nuns earned him a seven-year penance from Dunstan.

convents, which are instead supervised by his wife (number three).

At Wilton, the story splits in a way that should be familiar to you by now. The Goscelin/pro-Edgar version has it that, at Wilton, Edgar encounters Wulfthryth either with or without Wulfhild's connivance. In most versions he encounters Wulfthryth deep in study and is smitten. However in the pro-Edgar accounts she is a schoolgirl[24] and not a nun. The attraction is mutual and they run off together, Wulfhild being appropriately compensated. In the less Edgar-friendly versions, however, she is often already in vows and not always willing. Certainly, there is sufficient evidence that obtaining consent was not a priority for this, one of the last Anglo-Saxon kings. One way or another, with varying levels of enthusiasm depending on the teller of the story, Wulfthryth winds up pregnant in Kemsing, Kent, somewhere in the early 960s.

This is where, from our perspective, the story becomes interesting. Once again, like the princes-under-the-throne, the elopement with/abduction of the well-connected Wulfthryth had the potential to light the blue touch paper to some explosive political fireworks. This was not some servant girl or younger daughter of a minor family. Wulfthryth is seriously aristocratic. Moreover the children born to a king in successive marriages have the capacity to unsettle the succession, to trigger rebellions, and to die *suddenly* like Edgar's firstborn son, Edward. Instead, Wulfthryth walks away from the situation — whatever it is — after the birth of her daughter, Edith, with apparent goodwill on both sides. She obtains Edgar's acknowledgement of Edith, so that Edith is brought up as a Royal Princess, consulted by diplomats and bringing her own petitions to court, but protects her from the fallout of wife #3's ambition (which sees the terminal curtailment of the reign of Edith's half-brother, Edward, the son of wife #1).

Wulfthryth obtains from Edgar not only a significant full settlement, including *the Isle of Wight*, that she takes with her to Wilton, but two further grants to Wilton during her tenure as abbess. She then rules

---

[24] Yes, I know, not ok, but the bar is really low.

Wilton like a small kingdom, countering the officers of the King when she sees fit, but never provoking his ire or attempts to constrain her. She goes on to be an effective steward of the foundation of Wilton, remembered for generations with affection and reverence. To today's eye this may not seem like much of an achievement, but in an era when kings were assassinated and abbesses removed at the whim of well-connected people, her deftness in navigating the currents of power is remarkable. She is a force for peace and ably protects those for whom she is responsible. She has the tragedy to outlive her daughter by about 15 years, dying at the turn of the 10th century.

With the exception of Pocahontas, none of these women have stories of derring-do, or stand out particularly in a world of hagiographies in which evil is conquered and faith triumphant, but they deserve more. Again, these are 'well-behaved' women, which is not all the same as to say they were pushovers. Their stories generally aren't highlighted — they're certainly not celebrated in the current Church of England calendar — because they are not exciting. None of them are the principal actors in the stories of which they are part. Theirs are stories not of conquer and triumph, or of rebellion and ferocious integrity, but of keeping the ship afloat. They do not risk their lives, but neither do they imperil anyone else's. In fact, because of them, people stayed alive and solvent who might otherwise have gone to the wall. These are women who see the world as it is and meet its challenges with wisdom, faith and discretion.

To celebrate women like Wulfthryth and Pocahontas is to celebrate the peacemakers. It is to celebrate the people who stay out of the limelight, but keep an eye on the big picture. Theirs is a response to the Prince of Peace which speaks of service and attending to the common good: the diaconal traits of One who came to serve.

Scholars

Wulfthryth's daughter, **Edith**,[1] is a very different creature from her mother: not so much of a discrete personality. She is born in the royal manor of Kemsing, Kent, and taken to Wilton Abbey while still an infant. The fact that she takes the veil while still very young has led to certain assumptions by chroniclers of a patriarchal bent. One rather splendidly irritating description of her reasons has it that she went to Wilton, *"knowing not the world, rather than having forsaken it."* I'm not entirely sure how anyone could read an account of her life and come to that conclusion except with a very blinkered and determined set of presuppositions. Edith's mother, remember, does not hide Edith. She makes sure that Edith is very much present, if not physically, then in the political currents of the Royal Court. Edith is brought up well conscious of her royal status. She is educated by a succession of tutors appointed by her royal father, King Edgar, at least two of whom were imported from the continent. She has access to the King and to ambassadors and she dresses not like a nun, but like a princess, even wearing cloth of gold. When her brother Edward is murdered, by some accounts she is considered a possible successor. She is not to be messed with, not in life nor, as the stories had it, in death.

Edith is born somewhere in the early 960s, no later than 965 A.D. and she dies in 984 A.D., not making it to her 25th year. The ecclesiastical tides were changing and there was an increasing desire to differentiate between the capacities of men and women. This was the age when the Saxon abbesses were being constrained and hobbled, brought more tightly under episcopal control. Women were increasingly depicted as incapable of spiritual discipline or intellectual rigour. The growing cult of the Blessed Virgin Mary

---

[1] also known as Eadgyth, Editha or Ediva, of course.

was beginning to bifurcate women's identity into the binary choice of Madonna or whore. Yet Edith refuses to choose, refuses to be defined within a shrinking role. She is certainly not going to be constrained by other people's expectations or stereotypes. When Æthelwold, Bishop of Winchester, rebukes her for her vanity she tells him not to judge by outward appearances, "For pride may exist under the garb of wretchedness; and a mind may be as pure under these vestments as under your tattered furs". Like I said, she is not to be messed with. The same irritating author quoted above explains Edith's refusal of the post of abbess as "choosing the place of Martha." I suspect, rather, that she had more important things to do, like run her zoo and study.

The small number of organised religious houses that remained in Edith's time were not the intellectual powerhouses that we saw in the seventh and eighth centuries, but they were still centres of learning, holding significant libraries and responsible for the education of the female aristocracy. Edith was not the only one of an influential family to be brought up at Wilton. It was one of a cluster of convents within striking distance of the royal house of Winchester (which consisted between them of the majority of religious houses for women in England at the time). By now, England is united under a single crown: the one worn by Edith's father and then her half-brothers. Wilton in the 10th century strongly resembled a finishing school where the daughters of the aristocracy were both trained to run considerable estates and kept safe from the likes of Edith's father. ('Marriage' by kidnap was a standard practice, though not really approved of, like wifebeating in the 70s.) Once again, like our Kentish abbesses, we see our heroine creating connections that will carry her reputation across the south of England.

Even today, I think, the assumption remains that such women, remarkable, confident and well-dressed, who enjoy the good things of life (like keeping a menagerie or having hot baths), cannot really be devout. I have, for example, spoken to a number of women who have assumed that an enjoyment of clothes, jewellery and hairstyles is a contra-indication to any real vocation. Carter, whom we'll meet shortly, is another example of a woman who combines in her own person sincere faith and sartorial elegance. Edith's biographer, Goscelin,[2] is certainly aware of the discomfort and attempts to address it. He holds plenty of evidence that the young Edith is more than just a socialite.

The sisters that are Goscelin's main source point out to him where Edith habitually sat to read and pray. She is affectionately nicknamed 'Goda,' a common name which meant, 'the good.' And the sisters show him an alb which Edith embroidered with a picture of herself as a supplicant at the feet of Christ. The reason Edith opens this chapter — aside from the fact that she is simply obviously, brilliantly, clever — is that one of the most telling pieces of evidence for her personal faith is a prayer book that she composes and illustrates. Goscelin, writing her biography a hundred years later, is familiar with it, and the sisters of Wilton continue to use it for more than a hundred years after his time. This is a prayer book that reflects thoughtfully on Scripture and experience. It is a book laden with Edith's consciousness of her spiritual frailty.

Edith is also an artist. Not only do we have her alb and prayer book but we have, through Goscelin's eyes, the church she commissions, the decoration of which is one of the last things she organises before her death. The walls, Goscelin says, are covered in paintings of her design. He adds, "it is still so beautifully painted throughout the whole interior that it is more striking when seen than in any description". She dies within weeks of the church being dedicated to Saint Denys, her favourite saint. (Denys, by the way, was a clever chap, a famous preacher, and the first church dedicated to him in Paris was also built by a woman.)

A word of warning. If you doubt my assertion that she was both brilliant and devout, take heed from the experience of King Cnut. He is said to have doubted her sanctity, on the grounds that she was Edgar's daughter (an understandable cause of concern, Edgar being the letch he was). He has her coffin opened, whereupon she sits up and punches him on the nose. In some versions she keeps hitting him until he

---

[2] Yes, him again. I've come to the conclusion that he was the Agatha Christie of hagiographies in the 11th century. He just seemed to churn them out like pot-boilers.

acknowledges her to be a saint. Like I said, she is not to be messed with — in life or death.

Edith isn't unique, though. Let me draw your attention, once more, to Probably-Goda, her wall of learned women and the beautiful Book of the Gospels attributed to her. There was a solid tradition of artists, scribes and scholars that filled the religious — and occasionally private — houses of women for nearly a thousand years. Men and women read copiously, created a vast catalogue of manuscripts, which they decorated in a style that varied from earnest to whimsical to wildly (and wonderfully inaccurately) guessing what creatures like elephants and eagles might look like. Their scholarship was extensive and their learning profound. 99% of these people did their work anonymously and we will never know their names, but the assumption that it was only the men who populated the libraries of the Church is grossly mistaken. In the mid-eighth century Leoba (a woman of great renown, abbess of Bishchofshiem) studied, we are told, under 'learned abbess' Eadburh of Thanet. Those abbesses were still acclaimed for their scholarship centuries later, even if it was reframed. And women in these 'reformed' 10th century houses were still scribes and scholars.

See the **Old English Illustrated Hexateuch**, for example, produced for St Augustine's, Canterbury, shortly after the death of Edith's mother, Wulfthryth. Although much of the translation was done by the Benedictine monk Ælfric, there's evidence that it was illustrated, in part at least, by women. It has an extraordinarily high number of women in the marginalia, consistently through the document. Remember the walls of Canterbury Cathedral, populated almost entirely by men? We can be fairly sure that no one was just drawing women for the sake of gender balance. Its possible that, with a lay/unspecialised audience, the illustrator was assuming a female audience, but the odds are good that even then, we'd not be seeing quite so many women unless the artist had a female perspective.

The illustrations are fascinating because they give a relatively rare women's view of late Anglo-Saxon England. Every level of Kentish life — religious, secular, clerics, men, women — are drawn into the marginalia. Mothers, unlike in many manuscripts, are drawn as social creatures, rather than just biological functionaries. They are not just breastfeeding or giving birth, they are standing in family groups and interacting with their families as significant and integrated members of their households. We see both parents looking after the children (shock!) rather the seeing the usual men-over-here-being-interesting | women-with-the-children arrangements. The women in OEIH are lively, integrated people, often supplementary to the text in question (unlike the walls of Canterbury itself, where only strictly necessary women are painted). This manuscript is almost certainly copied and illustrated by women, for women. It is a thing of beauty. It is a piece of scholarship and artistry.

The 16th century dissolution of the monasteries was thus a disaster for women's education and intellectual credibility. There was no longer any point in educating women for a possible life in the academia of the religious life because that life had vanished. Although in the initial fervour the Renaissance women like Anne Boleyn and Margaret More were well educated, this inclination faded away through the next century. The narrative that women were defective, permanent children ruled by their emotions and their physicality, took over. Men were seen as superior both physically and intellectually and the Aristotelian perspective of women being born for the service of men dominated. Women were made by God for marriage and nothing else.

Thus the education of women was seen as wasteful, but also papist, having to do with a vision of women existing independently from men in religious houses. When Mary Astell (born 1666) tried to found a college for women she was accused of trying to set up nunneries on the sly. (Although her vision of it being funded by the contribution of women's diverted dowries, just like monasteries, really didn't help.) Fully 90% of women were left illiterate or semi-literate, equipped to follow the household accounts and the Prayer Book and no more. Many of them were discouraged from even discussing God, as a subject out of their sphere.

> *"Why therefore should these few among us, who are Lovers of Learning, although no better account cou'd be given of it then it's being a Diversion, be denied the Benefit and Pleasure of it, which is both so innocent and so improving?"* (Elizabeth Elstob)

Elizabeth Elstob is a friend of Astell, although a generation younger. She is born in 1683 in Newcastle upon Tyne in a well-educated family. As a child, her mother and her elder brother, William, encourage her to learn not only literacy but languages, and she excels. Tragically Elstob is orphaned at eight years old, causing a hiatus in her education. Elstob is sent to live with her uncle Charles Elstob, a Prebendary at Canterbury Cathedral. He puts a stop to her studies, having Views on the education of women. Nevertheless his Francophone wife, Matilda, continues to give her French literature to read and Elstob extracts what learning she can from an arid environment.

While Elstob is cloistered with her uncle, her brother goes to Oxford with a view to ordination. There he encounters George Hicks, the famous non-juror and, more importantly, a scholar of things Anglo-Saxon. Brother Elstob becomes part of a little Oxford set of Saxon scholars. In 1703 William becomes the rector of the joint benefice of St Swithin's and St Mary's in Bothow, London. This parish being in the gift of Canterbury Cathedral, there is a fighting chance their uncle Charles is involved in getting him the living. Some accounts have Elstob joining her brother while he is still at Oxford, but the balance of probabilities suggests that she would have waited until he had a household of his own. Either way, as soon as she has left Canterbury, Elstob's studies begin afresh and now she is mixing with her brother's Oxford set. She quickly masters Old English. The Elstob house becomes a Saxonist gathering house, attracting a range of the London intelligentsia including the high-profile (and devout) feminist Mary Astell. The younger Elstob is a well respected member of the set. The scholar Humphrey Wanley pays her five guineas for a copy of the Textus Roffensis[3], which is today generally considered one of the finest examples of its kind. (In 1753, nearly 35 years later, it was part of a collection sold on to the Nation for £10,000.) Wanley[4] describes Elstob as, "that ingenious virgin gentlewoman," and he collaborates with her on a regular basis, finding a place for many of her writings in the Harleian Library (an extensive library of manuscripts collected by Lord Robert Harley now held in the British library).

Elstob is perhaps best known for her work translating the Old English Life of Pope Gregory the Great by the Benedictine monk Ælfric of Eynsham (that same who translated OEIH). This is a truly beautiful work, with ornaments and engraved initials. It's an outstanding book, full of textual notes and a complete translation on the facing pages. What makes it really remarkable is the preface that she writes. In it she is determined to plot a spiritual genealogy of women, a line of authoritative female figures through the English Church. Using her dedication to Queen Anne as a springboard she lists a line of queens she describes as pivotal to the English faith. The opening initial 'I' is illustrated with portraits of saints Helena, Bertha, and the Virgin Mary as well as Queens Elizabeth and Anne, whose significance she lauds extensively.

This enables her vigorously to defend female learning, quoting from the Church Fathers' defence of the same. She argues that learning is good for the soul of both men and women, as well as equipping them with logical, ordered thought for the undertaking of their duties however lofty or domestic. She also accuses men of being "Admirers of Ignorance," who are not able to bear any woman to be better educated than themselves.

Having emphasised the 'liberties' of the English Church given by Gregory (via Bertha) to Augustine (carrying this through to look at Hilda at the the Synod of Whitby), she returns contemporary politics. She

---

[3] There isn't time to go into the significance of the Textus Roffensis here, although I touched on it in chapter 5. It was an ancient law code spliced onto a thorough inventory of Rochester Cathedral. It is a very beautiful window onto Anglo-Saxon and early Norman Kent, to which we have better access because of Elstob. We know she had her hands on the original, because she thought to improve it by *adding to the then 500 year old manuscript* a key to the Anglo-Saxon script!
[4] Humfrey Wanley (1672-1726), librarian and scholar of some note.

connects Gregory's purchase and liberation of the Anglian slaves with slavery practised by British plantation holders. These slaves, too, she says, should be liberated both from their literal shackles and also the figurative ones of ignorance and paganism. She is adamant that the slaves in the New World ought to be freed and educated both academically and in the faith of the people who had forcibly relocated them.

Her critic Thomas Hearne is so incensed by her eloquence that he manages at the same time to condemn the work as a "farrago of vanities" (how dare she address both politics and religion) but also to allege that the work is too well researched to be hers, and must be the work of her brother.

In the space of a dozen years she publishes this as well as an edition of the Latin Athanasian Creed with Old English notes, the first ever Old English grammar written in modern English, the copy of the Textus Roffensis for Humphrey Wanley, a further pamphlet on women's scholarship and begins the extensive work of attempting to produce a complete edition of Ælfric's Homilies. She is prolific and brilliant. But in 1714 Queen Anne dies, and Elstob is not the only woman whose academic credibility is severely crippled by her loss. Elstob dedicates subsequent works to other scholar-Queens — first Sofia of Hanover and then when she dies before publication to Wilhelmina, Princess of Wales — but to no avail. Then the following year her brother dies, taking with him her economic and social viability, and finally her principal academic patron also dies, the last straw for her academic career. She never completes her work on Ælfric's Homilies.

Elstob is now entirely alone and vanishes into the shadows. The fragility of her place at the edge of male patronage is exposed. At one point, a witness tells us, she is found in her rooms "surrounded by books and dirtiness." It is considered by many a fitting end for a woman who had aspired beyond her proper station in life and "pursued too much the drug called learning." Like her friend Mary Astell, Elstob makes ends meet by running a small charity school in a market town. For reasons that aren't clear, but might be deduced, she changes her name to Frances Smith. She's gone from being at the heart of an academic project in the centre of the London intelligentsia, to a shabby genteel woman, scratching a living. She vanishes from public life for some 20 years until she's found at last by friends. These same find her a place as a governess in the household of the grandchildren of her aristocratic patron, Lord Harley. I'm not sure how grateful she would have been. Certainly she had exhibited every sign of not wanting to be known in her obscurity. Perhaps the vulnerability of age made her more prepared to be a genteel servant in the house where she was once a scholar of national acclaim. She dies a nobody, in 1758.

This export of the Canterbury precincts is a woman who not only participates in the revival of Anglo-Saxon studies in this country, she's a crucial part of it. Moreover, she applies her studies to the issues of the day, to her understanding of herself as a woman of faith and conscience. In her writings she is generally trying to connect the life of her own Church in her age with that of the oldest church tradition in her country. She is almost as much of a church historian as a linguist. It should also not be forgotten that she set out to encourage and assist other women to discover the joy she has in the old Anglo-Saxon texts. Her grammar written in 1715, just before her brother died, is a response to a conversation with the daughter of the Dean of Canterbury, Mary Stanhope. Stanhope expresses an interest in learning Old English so Elstob goes ahead and produces a grammar accessible to those who do not have a classical education — in her spare time, one assumes. She writes,

> "Our Earthly Possessions are truly enough called a Patrimony, as derived to us by the Industry of our Fathers; But the Language we speak is our Mother Tongue; And who so proper to play the Criticks in this is the Females?"

Despite the best efforts of the likes of Elizabeth Elstob and Mary Astell, Queen Anne's relatively short reign did little to improve the credibility of women's education. Writer after writer seemed to fall over themselves to dismiss women's intelligence and warn of the terrible harm that was done to them through education. Daniel Defoe, Jonathan Swift, Henry

Fielding all decried women's education, and Henry Fielding even fell out with his until then beloved sister when she got a taste for education and scholarship and began to make a name for herself. He barely spoke to her again. The overwhelming conclusion of society continued to be that women were best kept at home minding hearth, husband and children. Women, persistently, disagree.

Just as Elstob was disappearing into obscurity, another scholar is born not far from where Elstob was brought up: **Elizabeth Carter**. Carter is the eldest daughter of Dr Nicholas Carter and his wife Margaret, an heiress from Dorset. Dr Carter begins as a curate in Deal, before becoming Rector of Woodchurch and Ham. He is one of the Six Preachers in Canterbury Cathedral. Clearly a brilliant man in his own right, he masters a number of classical languages while studying at Cambridge. All reports of him are of an agreeable, kind, devout and intelligent man. Unusually, for his time, he chooses to educate all of his children, all of whom seem to have been born extraordinarily talented — with the possible exception of Elizabeth Carter.

Carter is born in 1717 in Deal. Her mother dies when she is just 10, having apparently gone into a Decline after losing her fortune in the South Sea Bubble. Carter is left to be brought up by her father who sets about giving to his children his principal treasure. As an adult, Carter's younger sister is very kindly described as 'not a scholar' but still lively, with plenty of 'wit'. (She speaks only five languages.) As a child, on the other hand, it is Dr Carter's eldest daughter, Elisabeth, who is not considered the natural scholar. Her nephew, Rev Pennington later writes, "She gained the rudiments of knowledge with great labour and difficulty."

The need to excel that is to be one of her pre-eminent characteristics drives her to study in the teeth of her father's entreaties to stop. Her nephew describes how she would study through the night, using wet towels, snuff and alarm clocks to keep herself awake, as well as *eating* both tea and coffee. She wrecks her health (although this doesn't prevent her from living until 19 February 1806, making very nearly 90 years on this earth) but she achieves a level of scholarship that, in her time, makes her the talk of the country. Samuel Johnson, a man whose reputation as a writer and moralist carried him into the Church of England calendar of saints, said he knew no one better at Greek than Carter.

By the time she is done, she has mastered Latin, Greek, Hebrew, French, Italian, Spanish, German, as well as acquiring a working knowledge of Portuguese and Arabic. She is a first rate historian and astronomer, while being merely good at maths and music. She seems to have had a genuine enjoyment of needlework, while her mastery of cooking is sheer bloody-mindedness. Her skill at the fine arts, you might be slightly reassured to know, is merely ordinary. She has her first poem published at aged just 17, which becomes a steady flow of poems, pamphlets and translations in a wide range of subjects. Although she has an international reputation by the time she is in her early 20s, she is most famous for her translation of Epictetus. This work she began as an exercise of intellectual pharmacy for her friend Catherine Talbot. It took three years, to be published five years after its completion, in 1758, the year Elstob dies. It is a bestseller, earning her £1000 by public subscription from its first edition. There are three more editions of it in her lifetime, and it continues to be the default translation until the 1950s.[5]

Carter meets Catherine Talbot through her friendship with the Rookes of Canterbury who introduce her to the London scene. There, she encounters other like-minded women in a network of educated, intelligent women called the Bluestockings. These women make it their business to combine education with respectability. They are pious, socially conservative and politically neutral, a new kind of sisterhood: mutually supportive and mutually accountable, strongly aware of themselves as a 'gender identity' and conscious of the representative quality of their place in public life. They constantly remind one another of their duty to represent their sex well.

---

[5] That's not a typing error: her text was still the principal one until only 70 years ago.

This is the background to Johnson's famous quote that, "My old friend Mrs[6] Carter could make a pudding as well as translate Epictetus from the Greek, and work a handkerchief as well as compose a poem." This slightly backhanded compliment is the fruit of the Bluestockings persistent campaign to demonstrate that educated women do not necessarily run amok. Although Carter remains determinedly single her whole life, declaring to her friends that she did not have time to look after a husband and study (she regularly rose before 5 o'clock in the morning and rarely went to bed before midnight in order to maintain her discipline of study with the social life that she already had) she nevertheless makes a point of proving that she can indeed cook a pudding and embroider a handkerchief. She is known for her dancing and her wit at the many parties she attends. She is explicitly, deliberately, both 'feminine' and educated.

This does not mean that the group's public piety is a sham. Like Edith, Carter is both stylish and devout. Her translation of Epictetus is less a translation and more an interpretation. Woven into the text is her reflection on the common ground of Christianity and Stoicism, as well as their marked divergence. In her correspondence with her friend Talbot, both women are anxious that the translation should "lead its readers to Christ and not to Pagan Stoicism." She writes to another friend, Elizabeth Montague,

> *"The understanding of the Athenians was enlightened by philosophy... but their hearts were the hearts of barbarians. A sad proof that something more... is necessary to dispel the darkness of disordered principles."*

It is worth noting, I think, that compared to her contemporary, Samuel Johnson (did I mention that *he* made it into the Church of England calendar?) she is both more successful intellectually and more consistent in the application of her morals. Time and time again she is found speaking well of the people around her, or *tactfully* of the likes of Charles Savage, of whom she clearly does not approve. While Johnson

---

[6] Until recently Miss/Mrs functioned much more like Mlle/Mme, in that they were indicators of age much more than marital status.

is occasionally shown to display sour grapes at other people's success over his own, Carter is unfailingly gracious. (Granted, some of this is surely down to the determination of her set to navigate the public sphere with as much good credit to their sex as possible. It does not thereby diminish her self-control or the implication that it represents the good practice her religion.)

Like Edith, Carter's life is socially and intellectually brilliant, and that brilliance is laced through with the indications of her sincere piety. Her studies and her religion are not two separate spheres, but rather two conversational partners, each of which informed the other. The study of Scripture is "her constant care and greatest delight," and in an increasingly secular age she nevertheless seeks the comfort of the sacraments when she thinks she is dying. The local clergy bring their sermons to her before they preach them and she consults the bishops in her circle in her interpretation of ancient texts.

Her piety brings her joy, in the main. Her nephew writes that for Carter, her studies further open for her the Book Of Creation[7] so that "it was one of the great and striking proofs of the goodness of God, that so many objects of nature were capable, from their beauty as well as use, of imparting so much, and so perfectly innocent, pleasure." While she regularly deflects the often over-ornate compliments she receives, she does so with good humour and with a display of the very intelligence for which she is renowned. Admittedly, many of the texts she translates she also bowdlerises into moral and pious texts, but this filter enables the same texts to be made available in ladies' drawing rooms in a way that would not have been permitted otherwise. She, and the other Bluestockings, succeed in further opening the door of learning to their sex.[8]

---

[7] "... there is a great book: the very appearance of created things. Look above you! Look below you! Read it. God, whom you want to discover, never wrote that book with ink. Instead, He set before your eyes the things that He had made. Can you ask for a louder voice than that?" Augustine of Hippo

[8] Mary Wolstencroft, born shortly after Carter's publication of Epictetus, publishes *Thoughts on the Education of Daughters* in 1787 and *A Vindication of the Rights of Woman* in 1792, when Carter is in her seventies.

In stark contrast to Carter, **Simone Weil** doesn't give a flying monkey what anybody else thinks. Weil is born in Paris, in February 1909 the daughter of a French Jewish doctor. She is a woman of contradictions. Born into an affluent family, she is convicted by an intense concern for the very poorest in her society. Raised an atheist and an intellectual, her life's path is one towards mysticism and asceticism. Both of these drives seem to be compounded by an alienation from her own body which might be traced to a childhood illness and ongoing ill-health. She is obsessively hygienic, revolted by anything she considers dirty, and loath to be touched. She rejects her femininity as a distraction from more important things, fearing it makes her less credible. She is also a pacifist, who insists on fighting in the Spanish Civil War. She is a communist who denounces Stalin; a Christian convert who corrects Rome.

Like her brother, the mathematician André Weil, Weil is intelligent beyond the usual. As a child she conquers Greek, and when, later, she decides she needs to read the Bhagavad Gita she learns Sanskrit, like you do. She gains an entrance to the Lycée Henri IV that is rare among her sex at the time, and when she earns her Certificate of General Philosophy and Logic (second attempt) at the close of the 1920s, she is second in her cohort. She goes on to achieve her DES (diplôme d'études supérieures, roughly equivalent to an MA) at École normale supérieure in 1931.

It is a mark of Weil's obsessive dedication that she consistently, from childhood until her death bed, engages in a sort of performative socialism analogous to that of the Old Testament prophets. As a child during the First World War she refuses sugar when she finds out that the soldiers have none; as a teacher in the 1930s, she takes a year's leave to experience life on the factory floor (she describes it as little better than slavery); as a refugee in England she declines to eat a diet more substantial than that available to her compatriots back in Paris. This last, at the very least contributes towards her early death.

Weil has been accused of being a Gnostic, in part because of her self-alienation which never really leaves her, and in part because of her admiration of the Cathars (a Gnostic sect in 11th and 12th century France). Her resistance to baptism, as well as her emphasis on 'de-creation,' (which might more classically be described as *kenosis*[9]), leaves her open to the accusation of rejecting creation. This resistance to baptism is not a rejection of matter, but of philosophical commitment. She cannot wholly relinquish "the love of those things that are outside Christianity." Like Augustine of Hippo, she finds threads of gold wherever she looks, but unlike Augustine she has more difficulty integrating them into Christian thought. She is too much of an original to subscribe entirely to somebody else's description of the nature of reality. Nevertheless the body of her writings, in her conviction of the incarnation and the salvation that is to be found only in God, of the beauty of creation and the demands of our neighbour, she is profoundly Christian.

Weil writes of a radical self-forgetfulness wrought by 'attention.' "Attention is the rarest and purest form of generosity." This is why, for her, personal intimacy is a distraction from God, because it draws her mind and desires back to herself. She writes that beauty, friendship, liturgy are all hints of the divine, but that real love can only be established through radical self-denial, which is the only love that represents God. Self-denial, therefore, is what enables us to make room for God, just as God makes room for creation. For Weil, affliction and suffering are a training ground for self-forgetfulness, and consequentially provide the surest route to seeking God.

Although she says, "I never sought God; I was found," she does have clearest visions of God when she is trying to escape her own physical suffering. She comes to Christianity through a series of mystical encounters triggered — like so many mystics — by a combination of ill health and external stimuli. In her case it is severe headaches, and her attempt to distract herself from them with art, music and poetry. In 1938 she reads George Herbert's *Love* (III) while in the grip of one of her migraines. The fact that the poem is so transformative for her argues strongly against the Gnostic characterisation of her thought:

---

[9] Greek: κένωσις, kenosis: emptying – in theology: of the self

the poem is a highly sacramental and incarnational description of God's love, rooted in creation.

Her writing is prolific. When her family flees Nazi occupied Paris she writes a series of essays on subjects as diverse as scientific theory, political theory, the Renaissance, the criminal justice system, the ancient Greeks — all threaded through with her growing awareness of the divine. God, she believes, is the uniting force of society. When, at length, she lands in London in 1942, hoping to be recruited as a saboteur for the French resistance, she is asked by de Gaulle instead to draw up a plan of what the reconstituted French state might look like. The result is *The Need for Roots* (a document far too radical for de Gaulle to implement) which reads like a précis of her years of thought and social empathy. Like John Donne she describes the human race as being fundamentally interconnected; like William Tyndale she cannot forget the importance of the plough boy:

> *A lot of people think that a little peasant boy of the present day who goes to primary school knows more than Pythagoras did, simply because he can repeat parrot-wise that the Earth moves round the Sun. In actual fact, he no longer looks up at the heavens. This Sun about which they talk to him in class hasn't, for him, the slightest connexion with the one he can see. He is severed from the Universe around him.*

All Weil's life, therefore, she teaches. Just as she escapes her own physical affliction through poetry, she is convinced that education offered a path out of privation and suffering. Modern education, she argues, has become a thing of utilitarianism rather than being the love of Wisdom that it ought to be. Unlike her predecessors, Elstob and Carter, arguing that women should be educated in order to be freed from an entirely utilitarian existence, Weil is now arguing that education itself needs to be liberated from utility.

Like her life, Weil's death is surrounded by ambiguity. Because she refuses a better diet than is available to her compatriots under German occupation - even when she needs the nutrition to fight TB – there are many, including the newspapers of the day, who consider it suicide. Others call it a form of martyrdom, yielding her principals to no force, not even the disease destroying her lungs. She dies in a sanatorium in Ashford in 1943, aged 34 years. The death certificate records cardiac failure caused by malnutrition. Her tombstone, wholly unremarkable and hardly marked, not far from where she died, reads,

> "In 1942 Simone Weil joined Government the Provisional French in London But developed tuberculosis and died in Grosvenor Sanatorium, Ashford. Her writings had established her as one of the foremost modern philosophers."

For all of these women, Carter, Edith, Elstob, Weil, education — *Wisdom* — is the path to fullness of life, and to God herself. They are not just innovative they are *attractive* thinkers. They encourage others to see what they have glimpsed of the Glory of God. They are not ivory tower scholars, disconnected from their God or their neighbour. Their studies are part of the outworking of their faith: a celebration of the marvels of God, calling other women to see likewise and rejoice in the God who creates such wonders. They are wonderfully varied, passionate, dedicated and influential in the life of the Church, albeit largely unremembered.

The mediaeval depictions of Mary at the Annunciation drew her beside the written word as she was about to receive the living Word into her body. In the same way, scholars are an illustration for us of what it is to dwell upon the Word. Augustine of Hippo talked about the twin gospels: the Book of Life and the Book of Creation, both of which draw us into our understanding of the divine. These scholars of this chapter, by sinking themselves in the study of both these books, encourage us to do the same while helping us in the task.

This chapter has been longer than average, with more examples than I've normally offered, because in many ways these are the women least noticed in our Christian history. Do you remember that 4:1 ratio of men to women in our calendar of saints? Well, when I tallied up the people in our calendar described as, variously, teacher, scholar, moralist, spiritual guide or writer, the ratio[10] jumps to 57:6. That's nearly 10 times as many men recorded for their intellect, writing and teaching as women. (None of the women I've listed above make the cut, obviously.) This means there have been only six women in 2000 years that the Church celebrates as intelligent! It is indeed a category that the Church has found difficult to imagine: an intelligent but nonetheless exemplary woman.[11]

Theirs — Carter, Edith, Elstob, Weil *et al* — is a rich model of discipleship for women, of encouraging learning and study. They break the stereotypes of the clever woman being disengaged with the people around her, or socially inept. We have Carter who was at the heart of a fashionable social life and Edith who was well engaged in her political world, versus Weil who was clearly uncomfortable at parties, but was never content with theory divorced from practice. Weil's intellect, like Elstob's, led her to make sharp criticisms of social inequalities, having had her eyes sharpened to them by both nature and reflection. All of them spend their time searching both the Book of Life and the Book of Creation, partly for the joy of it, but also that other people might have better tools at their disposal for their own discipleship. All of them pushed open the door a little wider for others to come through. We deserve to celebrate them.

---

[10] This isn't a scientific study, you understand, but a quick canter through the lectionary with my index finger. I'm prepared to accept there might be seven women, on a recount, but then there might be 60 men.

[11] "Let such as say our sex is void of reason
know 'tis slander now, but once was Treason." (Ann Bradstreet 1643)

Social reformers

If I struggled to limit entrants for the previous chapter, this one concerns a genuinely rare breed: people who have changed how society is constituted. There are many in this book who might take the adjective 'reformer'. Our scholars, for example, might be described as reformers, because they have imagined that the world might be different than it is and described their vision, even, acted accordingly on an individual scale. Our Protestant Reformation Martyrs, similarly, were fired by an ambition for the Church Reformed. Eleanor Plantagenet and her husband also had a vision that they tried to implement nationally, building a foundation for the representative democracy that we have today. Others, like Gilmore or the early Kentish minsters, on the other hand, worked to change the lives of the people around them. They might be described as socially engaged, gripped with compassion for the poor, and mitigating their lot as best they can with charity, alms and education. Few, however, can be described as reforming *society*, for this is a behemoth of a task, to shunt society — that organic collection of mores and assumptions — off its chosen track and force it to look at what it does not wish to see.

It is indicative of the size of the task that, apart from Gilmore, these are the only women in this book who are recognised in the Church of England calendar of saints[1]. Theirs is both vision and energy in proportions very rarely found: to see a problem at the heart of society — in the criminal justice system, or how we treat our poor — and then to campaign for, and demonstrate a solution in such a way as to persuade a nation (and in Fry's case, a continent).

---

[1] but only since the turn of the century and only as commemorations. Yes, this is a chip on my shoulder. The more I look at the difference between the representation of men and women in our calendar, the crosser I get.

Both of the women in this chapter are cut from very similar cloth; both are activists while still in their teens, fighting prejudice and social stereotypes for the sake of those worse off than themselves. Both women exist on the fringe of the middle classes, which perhaps gives them the cultural capital to act while still being vulnerable enough to feel the needs of the people they seek to help: Elizabeth Fry is part of a religious minority, while Octavia Hill experiences relative poverty while still a child. Both these women have the misfortune to experience the social and economic embarrassment of bankruptcy (via the men on whom they are financially dependent).

Octavia Hill is born in Wisbech in 1838. She is introduced to social reformers at a young age, her parents being friends of the philanthropist Robert Owen. While Hill is only a teenager, her father is declared bankrupt and there is no extended family to rescue her and her mother from the poverty that follows. Her father, humiliated and depressed, abandons his family to fend for themselves. Her mother, Caroline, who seems to be a remarkably resilient young woman, moves to London to get work for her and her daughter. Caroline Hill sets up shop running a cooperative, and the teenage Hill manages one of the workrooms, staffed by children even younger than she. I struggle to imagine the social shock they had to navigate.

Hill is powerfully affected by the poverty of the children who work there. She organises meals and visits the sick, beginning a programme of nature-study walks around the local common land. This three-pronged response to poverty will be the hallmark of her work in London and surrounding counties.

Through her mother's connections, Hill begins to mix with the London social reformers and anti-capitalists, chief of whom is John Ruskin (for whom Hill worked as a copyist). It is Ruskin that buys the first set of houses that Hill manages on less than half the market profit. She insists that the houses are kept decent, with space available for the inhabitants to recreate. There is also a programme of education and culture, with the intention of enabling the residents to flourish. (By way of which Hill begins — in passing, as it were

— the Southwark Cadet Company, which will help form the Army Cadet Force. She is concerned for young boys she considers "past the age of make-believe" and thus, too old for Boy Scouts and the like.) By 1874 Hill is managing over 3000 houses in the capital. Eventually, she will be advising both the Ecclesiastical Commissioners and the London City Council in the management of their (slum) housing properties — and vigorously rebuking the Church's hard-heartedness.

It is shocking enough that the church owned such slums, but they were ubiquitous. Gilmore (we met her in chapter 2) who was just four years younger than Hill, describes in her reminiscences the state of the housing in London in the second half of the 19th century. She writes of whole families living on each floor of a tenement block, including families who lived their whole life in the cellar "skin blanched white from being in darkness so long". Hill herself, records the state of those first houses she bought with Ruskin: "The place swarmed with vermin; the paper, black with dirt, hung in long strips from the walls; the drains were stopped, the water supply out of order. All these things were put in order." *(Homes of the London Poor)* She is utterly scathing of the landlords and landladies — ecclesiastical or otherwise — who keep tenants in these conditions.

Another witness, a journalist, described a set of tenements as

>"*a court containing 22 houses... the basement storey of nearly all... was filled with fetid refuse, of which it had been the receptacle for years. In some... it seemed scarcely possible that human beings could live: the floors were in holes, the stairs broken down, and the plastering had fallen... In one, the roof had fallen in: it was driven in by a tipsy woman one night, who sought to escape over the tiles from her husband.*"
>(George Godwin, *The Builder*, 1859.)

The situation was crying out for remedy, but it seemed as if the problem was too endemic, too inevitable in the face of great swathes of the population entering the cities. And, as we shall see with prisons, no one knew where the money would come from to fix it. From Hill's initial encounter with urban poverty, in her mother's cooperative, she concludes and maintains that, "you cannot deal with the people and their houses separately." Over the years, Hill trains a small army of proto-social workers: women who manage the people in Hill's estates. The least of their work is to collect the rent, they are there to inspect the people and the property, to look for signs of abuse and to encourage the tenants in social cohesion.

Meanwhile Hill has become convinced that society's response to poverty is haphazard and inefficient. In 1869 she begins the Charity Organisation Society, which forms the basis of the Citizens' Advice Bureau (now the charity Family Action). This is an attempt to coordinate the work of several charities, ensuring communication and signposting between them. Unfortunately, it swallows whole the Victorian distinction between 'deserving' and 'undeserving' poor, causing it to be nicknamed "Cringe or Starve". It is born of the assumption that, if mishandled, charity leads to dependency, and is a vehicle for Hill's passionate determination to set people on their feet. (She was later to admit that the line was harder to draw than she thought.) For all its flaws, the Charity Organisation Society sets a standard for charity to be more than simply the scratching of a philanthropic itch, but rather for it to be something focused on the people who need help.

Indeed, it is a feature of Hill's work that she constantly emphasises, not just that poor lives matter, but that there is no such thing as 'the poor', but only human beings. All the relationships of charity, she believes, are two-way. It is necessary, she writes, to "trace the same tendency to good and evil in oneself" rather than simply point the finger at the twist of fate and moral failings. She returns, again and again to Thomas a Kempis' *Imitation*. It is the work of every Christian to make a gift of their own self, "following in your great Master's steps."

In 1877 her growing convictions about the nature of human flourishing leads her to set up the Kyrle Society, which forms the basis for the National Trust nearly 20 years later. She writes, "We all want quiet. We all want beauty... we all need space. Unless we have it, we cannot reach that sense of quiet in which whispers of better things come to us gently." *(Homes of the London Poor)* Not only do people need space, Hill is adamant, but they need places that they can afford to reach. In the case of Hill's tenants, this means somewhere they don't have to lose a day's pay to visit. It also requires people to be free to cross the land: Hill campaigns fiercely for the protection of public footpaths.

Having an eye both on housing and on public space, Hill sees the way the wind is blowing in the exponential growth of the cities. As well as protecting individual properties for public use, Octavia Hill begins to see the need to protect the countryside — or at least to stop the countryside being pushed too far away from the city centres where the poorest people are to be found. She coins the phrase 'greenbelt' in her campaign to protect Toys Hill and Ide Hill from development.

Eventually work, grief, and the end of a love affair, leads to something like a nervous breakdown in 1877. Her friend, Harriet Yorke, takes over much of the management of Hill's affairs. They take a cottage together in Crockham Hill so that Hill can benefit from the very space that she has worked so hard to make available for others. All her life, Hill, who disparagingly describes herself as a natural Martha, takes pains to remember and to forge in herself "that deepest way of work," the work, as it were, of Mary. She has for many years pushed against her own grain in the business of contemplation, pouring herself into meditations on *The Imitation of Christ*. She now has the space to practice it in earnest. She continues, nevertheless, to write and campaign and organise for another 30 years or so. She dies in August 1912, at the age of 73, and is buried with her sister at Crockham Hill.

Despite the strong overlap in their concerns, the chronological overlap of Fry and Hill is tiny. Hill is 7 years old when Fry dies in 1845. Their social overlap, on the other hand, is significant: both at the fringes of wider society but at the very heart of a socially galvanised milieu.

Elizabeth Fry is born Elizabeth Gurney, in Norfolk, 1780, around the time that Carter is settling into a slightly deaf old age. She is the third of 13 children in what we might describe as a nominally Quaker family, although her mother, Catherine Fry is a devout woman. Catherine Fry has a profound influence, but unfortunately for both women, a short one. She dies when Elizabeth Fry is 12 years old.

Although painfully shy, Fry is, like Hill, naturally politically and socially active. All her life she remains a woman of action, applying practical solutions to practical problems. By the time she is a teenager she is running a Sunday school and visiting the sick. She makes a friend of Amelia Alderson, whose family is involved in the Corresponding Society, a group working for universal suffrage. As an impressionable teenager, therefore, she rapidly becomes familiar with the ideas of Mary Wolstencroft, Thomas Paine and William Godwin. It speaks volumes for the kind of woman she is to become that this early encounter with republicanism leads her to ride through Norwich, brandishing the Tricolor.

This foundation of desire for political and social equality means that when she comes across the radical equality of devout Quakerism she is blown away by it. The spark that lit the fire that would drive her to transform the penal system of Europe is the Quaker speaker William Savage. She would afterwards write, "Today I felt there is a God. I loved the man as if he was almost sent from heaven — we had much serious talk and what he said to me was like a refreshing shower on parched up earth." She takes up a form of Quakerism described as being a 'plain Quaker.' This is quite a struggle for a young woman who delights in colourful clothes and extravagance. The story goes that the one trace of this in a life dedicated to Quaker principles is the brightly coloured laces that she wears in her boots.

Two years after her encounter with William Savage Fry marries a fellow 'plain Quaker', Joseph Fry, at the turn of the century. She has 11 children with him between 1801 and 1822. There is, therefore, an understandable interval between her marriage in 1801 and her recognition as a Quaker minister in 1811, but by 1813 she's again socially active enough to be contacted by a fellow Quaker, Stephen Grellet, regarding the state of women's prisons, and Newgate in particular.

Newgate Prison was one of the older London prisons and it had already been rebuilt twice in the previous century. It was built into the city wall, some five stories high, with a capacity for 150 prisoners but in reality containing many, many more people. Despite the Howard reforms that had required individual cells, the prisoners at Newgate were still kept in large dormitories called *wards*. Fry takes a small group of women with her to visit Newgate Prison and is comprehensively horrified. She finds 300 women in two rooms, sleeping on straw. It is a brutal mixture of convicted and remanded, adult and child, living and dead — with the dead children stripped of their clothes to clothe the living ones.

The prison service in England was well known to be shambolic and inconsistent. It still lent heavily on the Elizabethan Poor Laws which had first introduced the idea of Houses of Correction, but it was emphatically parochial. Two centuries of reform had slowly moved the culture of punishment from corporal to incarceration. While in the 17th century a sentence in the House of Correction would be for a matter of days, by the end of the 18th century a sentence of several years was becoming increasingly common, especially as transportation suffered a hiatus after American Independence. The infrastructure, on the other hand, had received no corresponding investment or organization. Penalties were administered via a haphazard system of gaols, Bridewells and prison ships. In addition, the wheels of criminal justice ground exceedingly slowly, so prisoners would sometimes be waiting years for trial, and then months if not years for sentence to be carried out. Conditions were decidedly insanitary, causing disease to break out on a regular basis, killing hundreds at a time.

Prison was a "dullsume Miserable Place," with little oversight. Prisoners were required to pay fees to the jailer for their accommodation, food, drink and 'privileges'. In addition, new prisoners were expected to pay a 'garnish,' or entry fee, to the other prisoners, the forfeiture of which could result in them being stripped naked. Violence and sexual assault were common. Then, when not fearing some form of assault, or worrying about paying their overheads, boredom became a perverse twin to anxiety. Prisoners had little to do to distract themselves from the fear of a death sentence or transportation.

The country as a whole was not ignorant of the state prisons — John Howard had written extensively about it some 30 years before Fry visited the prisoners at Newgate — but a series of pieces of legislation had done little to affect the majority of prisons. Nobody could agree who was to pay for it.

It's another three years before Fry's firstborn child is old enough for the Quaker minister really to take the bit between her teeth. (She whiles away the time by setting up a school for girls and organising a local vaccination programme, naturally.) When Katherine Fry (who we can only imagine was named for her grandmother) reaches 15 years old Fry begins visiting Newgate in earnest.

Crucially, Fry takes time to observe and listen to the women before she takes any action. She discovered of the women that, *"Want of employment, was the subject of their continual lamentation... They complained that they were compelled to be idle, and that having nothing else to do, they were obliged to pass away the time doing wrong."* The following year she sets up a small school for the children in the prison as well as rudimentary chapel facilities for the women, leading prayers and Bible study. She also creates the "Association for the Improvement of Female Prisoners in Newgate." This group of Quakers provides materials for the prisoners to work with and then sells the fruits of their labour on the prisoners' behalf. The transformative effect of education for the children and meaningful activity for adults is such that Fry is invited to address Parliament in 1818. She is the first woman to do so not wearing a crown.

Consequent to Fry's influence on Parliament, The Gaols Act of 1823 is passed, which states that "prisons should be made secure; gaolers should be paid; female prisoners should be kept separately from male prisoners; doctors and chaplains should visit prisons and lastly, *attempts should be made to reform prisoners*." (My emphasis.)

Having changed the law, Fry does not rest on her laurels. She spends a large portion of the rest of her life on tour, inspecting prisons, talking to reforming organisations across Europe, setting up visiting committees. She does not limit herself to conditions in prisons, but goes on to shine a critical light on mental asylums, workhouses and prison ships. Again and again she repeats her refrain of the need for dignity, education and purposeful employment. She also sets up the Brighton Visiting Society, an organisation with, for Fry, predictable themes. It is a nascent social work organisation, seeking to help the poorest in Brighton with — yes, you guessed it — education and purposeful work (with the overall intention of helping them regain their dignity). Here, as in her prison work, we can see the influences of Wolstencroft and Paine. Fry is determined that every individual should be valued and given dignity, so that they can find the *divine light*[2] within them. (Unsurprisingly, she also campaigns against the death penalty on the grounds that it only brutalises society.)

The late 1830s sees Fry set out to take her reforming principles to the governments of the Continent. (In her spare time, she also begins to campaign against the slave trade.) It is while she is in Germany, incidentally, that she encounters the Kaiserwerth Deaconess House that has such an impact on Elizabeth Ferard, who sets up the initial deaconess movement. Fry is also greatly impressed and also brings the practice back to her home country, setting up the Nursing House in London that was to supply Florence Nightingale with the women that she took to the Crimea. Just saying. Did I mention that during this time Fry finds time to set up a shelter for homeless people and a refuge for prostitutes?

Fry has, in recent years, been criticised for her relative social conservatism and a paternalistic approach to the women she sought to help. She is, true, for all her social fervour, a child of her age, with class-structured assumptions. Nevertheless, Fry does not seek to capitalise on the state of those worse off than her, but rather to improve their lot — with the assumption that

---

[2] This is the Quaker principle that everybody carries within them the light of God, which both allows them to distinguish good from evil, and also reveals our common humanity.

this will also improve their character. This crucial difference is what landed her on the back of the £5 note for 14 years (that and the transformation of prisons across Europe). From her own writings it is clear that what Fry did, she did as a faithful servant to her Lord. Fry was particularly convicted by that special vulnerability to which her own sex was exposed to should they find themselves in the institutions established for those on the margins,

> *"All reflecting persons will surely unite in the sentiment, that the female, placed in the prison for her crimes, in hospital in her sickness, in the asylum for her insanity, or the workhouse for her poverty, possess no light or common claim on the pity and attention of those of her sex who through the bounty of a kind Providence are able 'to do good and to communicate'."* (Observations on the Visiting, Superintendence, and Government of Female Prisoners, 1827)

It was Fry's constant endeavour to bring the Bible into the places that she visited, and to do her best to establish understanding of its contents. This has its effect. In her correspondence with the women she encountered, they consistently communicate their own understanding of the transformation they've experienced using the language of redemption. At the very least, this demonstrates their respect for Fry and for her motivations.

All this would have been phenomenal, accomplished by any human being. Fry established the principle across Europe that, "Punishment is not for revenge, but to lessen crime and reform the criminal." She is the more remarkable because she is not only part of a religious minority and a woman in a man's world (when women could neither vote nor attend university) but she is addressing subjects far outside the proper feminine sphere of home and hearth and virtue — and is nevertheless still listened to, still changes things, still lays down a marker of decency that is *still* referenced 200 years later. Add to this the persistent murmur of disapproval throughout her campaigning because she continues to have children into the 1820s, and refuses sit at home with the babies like a *proper* mother.

She begins her work as the wife of a successful businessman, but Joseph Fry hits the financial rocks in 1829 and becomes bankrupt. Unlike Hill, Fry's family are able to step into the breach and house the Frys, but the couple's credibility is damaged. Having lost the shield of wealth and financial success, Fry is attacked in the press for abandoning home and hearth for her dangerous ideas. Subscriptions to her campaign fall dramatically, but she persists. Having begun her campaign from a position of wealth and some social advantage, she continues it in the face of straitened circumstances and public derision.[3] Fry continues her efforts all her life, never resting from her campaigns. She sets up her deaconess-style Nursing House a mere five years before she dies. The year before she dies she is setting up a refuge for prostitutes.

Bearing and giving birth to 11 children also has its impact on her health, which is poor for most of her life. In the summer of 1845, after the death of her second son and his children, Fry spends some time in Ramsgate 'taking the sea air' in the hope of restoring her health. (She would have been familiar with the port town. She insisted on visiting every convict ship that carried female prisoners before it set off to the British colonies. Ramsgate was often the last stop in Britain before the prison ships, loaded with female convicts, set sail for New South Wales.) The convalescence does not work. Fry dies from a stroke in Ramsgate, on 12 October 1845, aged 65.

Should you still doubt that Elizabeth Fry was an extraordinary woman, I offer you this detail: this shy woman who hated social gatherings but nevertheless spent her life campaigning, travelling, talking to strangers (in the sense of people who were utterly strange to her, as well as those whom she simply did not know) this woman who committed herself lifelong to visiting some of the darkest and most oppressive

---

[3] Admittedly, the Queen and the Prime Minister, Robert Peel, thought she was quite something, which certainly helped her campaigning but they were in a minority. The louder, more persistent commentary on herself that Fry would have heard, was that of popular opinion, in all its derision.

corners of her society and investigating some of the nastiest boats this country has produced, this woman *was afraid of the dark and of the sea*.

Both of these women, Fry and Hill, were phenomenal in achieving on the national stage what Christians are routinely trying to do in their own environs. They were also significant in enlarging a little further that feminine public sphere that allows the voices of women to be heard. Neither woman properly matched the gender stereotypes their society set for them. Fry more or less left her large family to its own devices, while she travelled the continent arguing for a restorative, rather than a punitive justice system. Hill, on the other hand, simply wasn't the gentle, negotiating creature that the Victorians thought a women ought to be, but was rather routinely dictatorial and scathing. (William Temple, for example, described her address to the Ecclesiastical Commissioners: "She spoke half an hour... I never had such a beating in all my life.")

Hill and Fry are worth celebrating because they both worked from deep conviction, using both individual and institutional action to change the way society thought of itself. Theirs was a clarion call to action, heard by the movers and shakers of the country. It was not enough for them to restore the people they encountered, they wanted the country — and in Fry's case the Continent — to see the inherent humanity in the most vulnerable in society and act accordingly. They were giants among women.

Wives, mothers and daughters

If writing about all the unimagined women who have lived their Christian life in Kent, the women most unrecorded, most unconsidered are the ones who have simply lived their lives as wives, mothers and daughters. These are the women who, above all, 'do not make history'. For decades, even those history books which purported to give an account of the social and economic context for a period did not include the domestic and economic lives of women. Unfortunately, by the very nature of the exercise, this becomes a vicious circle. These stories, untold, are the hardest to tell.

We find traces of them in fiction, here and there. The great majority of these stories are some form of injunction for women to be meek and good and hard-working and pious — or as invective against the 'bad women'. One or two exceptions can be found, however. There is the *Ballad of a Tyrannical Husband* which gives a comprehensive list of the tasks expected of a mediaeval wife from the labouring classes. This list is recognisable, to most women, but in addition to the cleaning and cooking and childcare, there is the creation of clothing from scratch — not just sewing but first carding the wool/preparing the flax, spinning and then weaving — as well as making the butter and the cheese, and caring for the smallholding that was the garden. This is an unrelentingly hard life.

In Chaucer's *Canterbury Tales* we see perhaps the best known, most vivid depiction of a mediaeval wife in the 'Wife of Bath's Prologue'. The Canterbury Tales are a series of stories within stories told by a motley selection of pilgrims to Thomas Beckett's shrine. There is a nun, and a carpenter, a miller, a monk, a friar... and 'A Good Wif' from Bath, a maker of cloth and wealthy, with fine, gaudy clothes and a penchant for pilgrimages and religious festivities. No saint is she, but she is a striking picture of what it meant to be a married woman in 14th century England.

The Wife describes the misogyny of the standard portrayal of women, in a catalogue of the accusations brought against women and in the list of wicked women with whom they were regularly compared. She touches on the misery of a sexual partner she didn't choose (and that, at the age of 12) and on the violence from which she had no recourse, harsh enough to leave permanent damage.

> *"By God, if wommen hadde writen stories,*
> *As clerkes han withinne hire oratories, [ivory towers]*
> *They wolde han writen of men moore wikkednesse*
> *Than al the mark of Adam may redresse."*

It is a vision of marriage in which happiness is largely a matter of chance, and likely to be temporary. The choice of partner was either by a third party, or with a good chance of being ill-informed, since interaction between people of opposite sexes was severely restricted. Our fictional wife is an exaggeration with her five dead husbands and still on the lookout for a sixth, but life expectancy was short and the majority of people[1] married more than once. To be lucky in your allotted mate once was no guarantee the next time round. (This lottery is not limited to mediaeval wives: Elizabeth Bennett's best friend in *Pride and Prejudice* makes the same point.)

The prologue demonstrates the subversion of patriarchy, the use of its own arguments against it, not original to Chaucer[2], but this Wife, Alice, also argues hard for the intrinsic worth of marriage. She has no truck for the use of virgin 'purity' as a stick with which to beat married women. She uses the very imagery deployed by Jerome to illustrate the value of virginity — gold versus wooden plates — to point out that the wooden dishes are usually more useful. Time and again the Wife takes the weaponry of Scripture passages to point out all the holy patriarchs and kings who were married, and married repeatedly. True, she has a shaky distinction between successive marriages and infidelity, but her principal point is the rejection of double standards. Hers is a snapshot of

---

[1] The ones, that is, who weren't the partner who died first.
[2] See, for example, *The Book of the City of Ladies*

everyday(ish) life and faith, and of marriage in all its richness, cruelty and folly.

The Wife is not a self-pitying portrait — quite the contrary. The Wife of Bath shows a rich appreciation of marriage as a gift of God in creation. Perhaps most especially of the gift of her "queynte"[3] and the pleasure it brings, which she's adamant is a primary, created purpose of "our bothe thinges smale", and not a side-effect. It is an enthusiastically physical outlook, grounded in experience and clear eyed. It is not surprising that the poet Chaucer should, through his creation, emphasise the creative process as a holy thing, but the Wife of Bath describes marriage as a *vocation*. "God clepeth [calls] folk to hym in sondry wyse," she says. She is enthusiastic about her vocation, "In the actes and in fruyt of mariage."

The idea of marriage as a holy thing formed much slower than its alternative vocation of celibacy. It's not until the 10th century, under Charlemagne, when the continental king started to deploy the, to us, familiar routine of the public Royal marriage. He encouraged the 'chivalrous' idea of women as the 'animate treasure' who needed to be protected and cherished. Marriage-by-kidnap, and the corresponding abandonment of wives began to be frowned upon. Most importantly, marriage began to gain its use as a sign of order and stability, the first hints that it might be a divine institution. When marriage became a sacrament in the 12th century it still came as a bit of a shock to secular society. If you think the current ruckus over the definition of marriage is bad, you should have seen the outrage among the aristocracy when the Church told them their children needed to consent to a marriage. For the first time, marriage became about more than children and property. It started to speak of the love of God, of the Kingdom of Heaven. Only so could our fictional wife talk about her *vocation* to marriage.

Having said that the Church insisted that consent was a requirement for marriage, nobody really interpreted that as 'full and frank consent'. It took Matilda's daughter, Mary, *who was a nun,* ten years and two children to establish that she hadn't consented to her

---

[3] I'll leave you to take a punt on what that means.

marriage, and to return to her convent. It took Joan, 'the fair maid of Kent,' eight years and three papal injunctions to establish similar clarity. In fact, it was her husband who had to run the legal case because Joan was basically locked in a cupboard. Let me explain.

Joan of Kent is born in 1328 of Edmund, first Earl of Kent, who is the grandson of Edward I. Unfortunately, Joan's father fatally backs the wrong horse when the reign of Edward II becomes a bit murdery, and he is consequently executed. Joan becomes a ward of the Queen Mother. Serious things are expected of her conjugal alliance. However, at the age of twelve Joan, presumably having similar ideas to the Wife of Bath about the godly use of her 'instrument', runs off with Thomas Holland, a Knight of her household. Young Thomas seems to have been a good choice, despite his comparatively lowly stature. In the fullness of time he becomes a trusted member of the Royal Court, skilled in warfare and dependable. He is also patient and persistent, which is crucial to their happiness.

The trouble was that, although the Church had established that consent was a necessary part of marriage, and everyone was agreed that sex was definitely necessary, there wasn't a lot of clarity about when a sexual liaison was a marriage. Joan and Thomas agree, presumably, that this is a thing they want to do and then skip off to practice their godly gifts, but they struggle to produce witnesses, having done it in secret. Mummy and Daddy Kent — or rather Mummy and Uncle Kent — therefore proceed to marry Joan to the much more eligible William Montague. Mummy and Uncle Kent, and I'm guessing husband number two, William, are not disposed to accept Joan's liaison with our Tom as a marriage.

Thomas is strapped for cash, but still sets about raising the necessary funds to take the case to the Pope to establish that he has dibs on the fair Joan. Not without difficulty, Joan manages to get the message to the Pope that she had indeed intended to marry Thomas Holland and that he is the man she considers to be her husband. It says much for the relatively new doctrine of the sacramentality of marriage that Joan's stated intention is the deciding factor. Joan is declared to be married to Thomas, and her marriage to William is set aside.

Joan is married to Thomas for a further 11 years, and unusually for her time — but perhaps understandably, given their history — she lives with Thomas wherever he is, on campaign or in court. Between them they produce six children, five of whom make it out of childhood, which was pretty good going. During this time, as I say, Thomas acquires a solid reputation with the King and is made the Earl of Kent in 1360. (Joan is by now, among other things, Duchess of Cornwall, Countess of Kent and Countess of Chester.) Sadly, in 1360 he dies and Joan is back down to no husbands, having had one, then two, then one again over the last 20 years.

Unfortunately for Joan, the whole two husband confusion was very much considered to be her fault — I'm really not sure how. Perhaps she was considered sneaky to have conducted a secret marriage in the first place. Perhaps she was considered insufficiently forthright about the first marriage when the second marriage was proposed. Either way, when the Black Prince, Edward of Woodbridge, declares his intention to marry her, it is not a little scandalous. Especially since husband number two, the eligible and powerful William Montague, is still alive (and remarried). She is definitely a Dodgy Woman. Fortunately for the romance, England has just set out on what is to become the Hundred Years War (they're not calling it that yet). The King, consequently, has a serious cash flow problem, related to military funding. While Joan doesn't bring with her the foreign alliances that a crown prince might be looking for, the fact that she does provide three counties worth of wealth means that Edward's father, King Edward III, is prepared to look upon the match with a kindly eye, bigamy or no.

You'll be wondering by now why our Joan is an example of anything much, apart from a romantic disposition and a certain amount of determination, but here's where she gets exemplary. Joan's background is sufficiently dodgy that her prospective father-in-law seeks, not just one, but two papal bulls to confirm that she is eligible to marry and that her children with Edward will be legitimate. That's *three times* that sundry Popes have said, categorically (and expensively), that Joan is/was married to Thomas and not to William. Joan needs, therefore, to be The Good Wife™, not only for her own sake, or even for Edward's sake, but for the stability of the country in a time of war. And she is, she really is.

She marries the Black Prince in 1361, and it's practically a fairytale wedding. They are both in their 30s, both handsome, both in love. He is a war hero and she has raised meekness to professional standards. Edward calls her, "my dearest and truest sweetheart and well beloved companion." They are married for 15 years, five of which Edward spends dying slowly of something that never seems to have been satisfactorily diagnosed. During Edward's illness, when she could have become quite a political force, Joan remains as neutral as possible. Any duties that she conducts in Edward's place, she does very much as his proxy. They have two sons, only one of whom makes it out of infancy. That one, Richard, is declared king in 1377, aged 10 years old, the second of his name. It is a real credit to this "slippery woman" that during her marriage to the Prince of Wales (she's the first 'Princess of Wales', by the way) she has rebuilt her reputation for honesty and dependability — and discretion — so much so that there is no argument about her retaining the guardianship of her son. This, in a time when a child's need for their mother was by no means an axiom.

Now Joan morphs into The Good Mother™. She is the most important woman in the country. She is rich and important in her own right and she is the mother of the King. She is on good terms with the whole court. All her efforts go into supporting her young son in his role. Her first family is by no means sidelined, but neither does she use her position to advance them. She becomes the invisible diplomat, quietly smoothing over contention and mediating between the different powers in the court. She surrounds her son with loyal people who will support his interests and advance his causes.

Then comes the Peasants' Revolt in 1381. Joan is in Canterbury at the time, visiting the tomb of her late husband, the Black Prince, but on discovering that her son is trapped in the Tower of London, she immediately hoofs it back to London, directly through the path of the rebellion. Such is her reputation that she passes through the rebel army unmolested (they even provide her with an escort) and she joins Richard in the Tower. Once there, however, she does not take over but is content to be moral support. At this first real test of his kingship, Richard succeeds, if brutally, and Joan takes it as a sign that her little king is all grown up now. She hangs around long enough to ensure a good marriage for her son to Anne of Bohemia, daughter of Charles IV (Holy Roman Emperor) and then she steps back.

Joan surfaces one more time in Richard's court, which is to attempt to mediate a row between the king and his half-brother. This time her skills are insufficient to the task, or perhaps the time allotted to her is insufficient. She dies later that year in 1385. Rumour had it that it was the row between her children that broke her heart. She is buried with her first love, Thomas Holland.

Joan of Kent exemplifies why 99.9% of women who have the vocation to "the actes and ... fruyt of mariage" are invisible. Not only is it an occupation only really of interest to (male) chroniclers and historians when it *fails* (compare the interest paid to Joan's contemporary, Alice Perrers, Edward III's controversial mistress), but the likes of Joan actively avoid the limelight. They are encouragers, mediators, nurturers — and not just of the children. I cannot give you even any particular demonstration of her religion: even her personal piety is discreet. While most of the women in this book could have their story told under a variety of chapters, the women in this chapter are only visible because they are the wives or children of powerful men. The domestic witness of centuries of women within the household has gone largely unremarked, much as gravity and breathable air are seldom pointed out.

Not all wives are invisible, of course. Having an army at your back does make you significantly more noticeable. Having the same name as your opponent, on the other hand, makes everything a little bit more complicated.

Matilda of Boulogne, is born in 1103, the daughter of Mary of Scotland and Eustace III, the Count of

Boulogne. She is the granddaughter of that Margaret of Scotland who is celebrated on the 19th November as a philanthropist and reformer. Matilda is educated at the same convent that educated and housed our Edith, a little over hundred years before. Edith, by the way, was the half-sister of Margaret of Scotland's great granddad. In case you were interested.

Matilda's marriage to Stephen de Bois is one which brings Stephen significant land wealth in England — including parts of Kent — as well as an alliance to a powerful trading nation. (Boulogne has access to key ports into Europe.) The marriage is arranged when Matilda is only two years old. By the time it comes about she is 23 and the Countess of Boulogne (on account of her father deciding to divest his worldly affairs and enter a monastery). Despite its delay, the marriage is an extremely happy and affectionate one. To the best of our knowledge, both parties are faithful (relatively unusual in an age of royal bastards) and when Matilda predeceases Stephen, the king is described as being like a broken reed.

The first 10 years of their marriage are relatively uneventful, with the exception of the arrival into their lives of several pairs of pitter pattering tiny feet. In 1135, however, Stephen's uncle, Henry I, dies with no sons. He has a daughter in France, however, and she is declared his heir. Now, this is where it gets a little bit complicated because Henry's daughter is also called Matilda. Fortunately for us, in the way you'll be familiar with by now, this Matilda was occasionally known as Maud so we will be calling her Maud from here on in, for the sake of clarity. Because Maud is delayed getting back to England for her Coronation, because there are enough people who think monarchs need to be able to wield a sword and he is Henry's nearest male relative, and most of all, I think, because he can, Stephen hotfoots it to London and calls dibs on the crown of England. He's anointed king, appropriately enough, on 26 December 1135. Matilda is crowned the following Easter. (It's probable that the delay is on account of another pair of tiny feet brewing.)

Maud is understandably put out, but the problem is that Stephen has now been *anointed* king, so even though Maud has the better claim, and was even named Henry's heir, the country is fairly evenly divided between her supporters and his. By and large, sacramental actions can't be undone. This is unfortunate, because when Maud shows up with an army in 1138 neither side has an obvious advantage and the resulting civil war rumbles on for 19 years in a period pointedly referred to as The Anarchy.

Despite her husband having thrown something of a spoke in the wheel of the country, Matilda is more than a help meet, she is his trusted general, diplomat, adviser and mainstay. Stephen is charismatic, but Matilda is trusted and respected. When Maud's army takes Dover Castle in 1138, it's Matilda who rallies an army and takes it back. When Stephen is captured in 1141, Matilda takes over the campaign. Again she rallies an army, again in Kent, and petitions earnestly for Stephen's release, offering Maud everything she can think of: money, land, victory, even herself in exchange. Maud refuses, so Matilda marches on London and takes it.

Once she holds London, Matilda is able to persuade the Bishop of Winchester, Stephen's brother-in-law, to change his coat for the second time and rejoin Team Stephen. This is not well received by Robert of Gloucester, Maud's right hand man, who promptly hoofs it down to Winchester and lays siege. Matilda, whose army has now been significantly swelled by the addition of London troops, rocks up and liberates Winchester, capturing Robert of Gloucester in the process. Matilda now has an unquestionably better negotiating position and an exchange of prisoners follows. Maud doesn't succeed in getting the upper hand again, although she also categorically refuses to concede.

This oddly sweet couple (Matilda and Stephen, that is) have each other's back, and keep each other company for the full 27 years of their marriage. They have five children, one of whom is dedicated as a nun (in Higham — the same lady who was kidnapped for 10 years); they found two abbeys, one of which, in Faversham, is in thanksgiving for the peace accord of 1147; Matilda, further, establishes Saint Katharine's in what is now Lime Street, as well as a couple of temples for the Knights Templar. The period of Stephen's capture appears to be the only significant time they spent apart. When Matilda falls ill with a fever, in 1152, Stephen hurries to her side. There is nothing he can do, but he stays by her bed until she dies.

In 1553 Stephen agrees a compromise with Maud's son and new right-hand man, Henry FitzEmpress. It's as if all the fight has gone out of him. Stephen declares Maud's son his heir to the throne and then goes on to cast off this mortal coil in 1154, having survived his wife by only two years. The pair are buried together in the Abbey they founded in Faversham.[4] Matilda's epitaph, composed by Stephen, reads, "If ever woman deserve to be carried by the hands of angels to heaven, it was this holy queen."

The roles in this chapter aren't always romantic. **Margaret Roper** was by all accounts a dedicated wife and mother, but the relationship for which she is famously faithful is that with her father, Sir Thomas More. Margaret is born in around 1505 in London. She is the daughter of a Renaissance man, educated in Latin, Greek and French, in history, philosophy and rhetoric, geography, astronomy, arithmetic and theology. This is not a vision of feminism from Thomas More, it is a vision of humanism, individualism and the importance of education. Young Roper (née More) is not trained for any profession, she is educated to be a wife and mother within her full capacity to respond to the glory of God.

In 1521 she marries William Roper in Eltham, Kent. William Roper is a lawyer and family friend, but at the time the Mores don't have the dowry for the eldest of the More children. Instead, William Roper is offered bed and board for him, his wife and their children. I'm not sure how joyfully William Roper receives this setup, but his wife is clearly devoted to her father. The two of them, daughter and father, seem to have spent most of her life poring over one text or another, engaged in translation and hermeneutics. Even to this day it's not clear how much of Thomas More's publications are his work, or where his daughter's influence ends. It is an indication of how close she is to her father, that when she falls seriously ill in 1528,

---

[4] If you're wondering where the tomb is, the Puritans threw the bodies into the river when the Abbey was plundered in the 17th century, which, frankly, seems a little rude.

even to the point of being comatose, her father rushes to her bedside. He researches, and concocts his own treatment, and Roper recovers.

The Ropers live with Thomas More until he dies. It says much for her conviction and coherence, that William Roper, who was a Lutheran when they marry, is persuaded by her to return to Rome. Between 1523 and 1544 they have five children, all of whom are educated to the same standard as their mother. Roper's daughter, Mary, for example, also becomes a published scholar of some acclaim.

Roper is clearly an intellectual force to be reckoned with. When her first child is barely one year old she publishes a translation of Erasmus' treatise on the Lord's Prayer. (She's the first non-royal woman to publish a translation into English — under her own name, anyway.) Erasmus is impressed and describes her as the "Flower of all the learned matrons in England." He dedicates his own commentary on hymns to Roper. Unfortunately most of her work is lost, the only other extant writings we are confident are hers are her letters to her father in prison.[5] On the face of them they are letters trying to persuade her father to change his mind and sign the Oath of Allegiance — Roper's justification for seeing her father in prison — but there is a suspicion that the letters, and their responses, were composed with her father by way of apologetics.

Eight years after Roper's marriage, Thomas More becomes Chancellor. (One memorable description asserts that he "took his job seriously and had heretics burnt at the stake." If it was only his position driving his pursuit of heretics, he did indeed take his duties seriously, even eagerly.) In a McCarthy-esque age, however, when thought crime is a thing, Thomas More is not immune. His relationship with Elizabeth Barton (chapter 3) has left his reputation tainted. When the King demands More's signed oath affirming royal control of the Church, Thomas More has no credit with which to negotiate.

In 1534 Thomas More is arrested and imprisoned. It is his daughter who is given access to him in the

---

[5] Even these, some commentators argue are in fact her father's work, of course, and admittedly his influence is manifest.

Tower. She is able to exchange correspondence with him, on behalf of others as well as herself, and carry out his papers (discreetly) for publishing. Then, in November, Thomas More is moved into solitary confinement, but for the first third of 1535 Roper continues to conduct clandestine correspondence with her father.

Roper meets her father for one last time on 4 May 1535. On 1 July he is tried and convicted. The story goes that on his way back to the tower, Roper is waiting on his route for one final farewell. Thomas More is beheaded on 6 July and his head is impaled on a spike on London Bridge, not quite a year after Barton's. Roper's persistent allegiance to her father during his time in prison was risky enough — treason and heresy are both considered infectious complaints — but she goes further. Rather than let her father's head be thrown into the Thames when it had finished rotting on the bridge, Roper manages to bribe the relevant person and retrieve it. (I wouldn't say pickling that head was the most routine of instincts, but each to their own.) She also saves her father's books and papers from the kind of fiery retribution often meted out to nonconformist texts.

It's not known why Margaret Roper died, only that she died a young woman, not quite 40, in 1544. In her lifetime she had worked hard at collating and curating her father's writings. After her death her widower and children continue the work of polishing Thomas More's reputation. She is originally buried in Chelsea, but when her widower dies 33 years later (he never remarries), her remains are moved so that she, William and her father's pickled head are all laid to rest at Saint Dunstan's, Canterbury.

In a Church which describes itself as the bride of Christ, and which often describes Jesus' mother as most holy purely on the grounds of her maternal role, wives and mothers are surprisingly ignored as patterns of faith. In fact, while for centuries women have been most encouraged to be wives and mothers, and dutiful daughters, there are extremely very few women who are celebrated for doing just that. I can only think of a tiny handful of saints[6] remembered for their sacrificial love of family, and one of them — Margaret Clitherow — is only in the Roman calendar. Part of the matter, I suspect, aside from the general lack of interest by churchmen and historians, is that when women are noticed as good wives, mothers, daughters, it is inevitably not their story. They are only ever the supporting actor in somebody else's drama.

Yet this very fact makes them, in many ways, the perfect pattern for discipleship. The very thing which seems to contribute to their sidelining in the history and celebration of Christian witness — that they are self-effacing, that they are not the centre of their own story — is the very thing for which we should all be striving.

Likewise, this familial love, the love which nurtures and supports and encourages, is at the heart of our understanding of the Godhead. The self-effacing love of the likes of Joan of Kent speaks of that action of God in our lives which we scarcely notice. The faithfulness of Margaret Roper, the courage of Matilda de Boulogne, placed at the disposal of their families, within the context of a life of faith, encourages us all. The invisible tending of a child in the womb mirrors the nurturing of the Word in the life of the believer. This is not necessarily *exciting* holiness, but then nobody wants gravity to be exciting, nor the air that we breathe. This is the holiness that puts the dinner on the table, that stops the wheels from coming off. Life is very much harder, and bleaker, without it.

---

[6] The Blessed Virgin Mother, Helena (Constantine's mum), Monica (Augustine of Hippo's mum) and Margaret Clitheroe — and Monica and Helena are both doubtful candidates for 'self-effacing' as an adjective. Interestingly, Rufus' mother, commended by St Paul, doesn't even get a name, which is typical, and says it all, really.

Virgins

While women putting dinner on the table may never have been something which has created religious acclaim or hagiographies, the ancient lists of the saints of the Church *are* full of women whose principal claim to holiness seems to be that they didn't have sex even when powerful men wanted them to. A proper female saint, for most of the writing of church history, has been the virgin martyr — the more brutally martyred the better. Run your eye over the hagiographies of virgin martyrs and you will find much nakedness and vulnerable flesh (but never rape or shame). Margaret of Antioch is a perfect example, a woman who is flayed, boiled, burnt, imprisoned, *eaten by a dragon*, and then eventually decapitated[1], all as some weird incel attempt at courtship. In Kent, we lacked martyrs so the best we could manage was chaste aesthetes — although the temptation to insert into the narrative slightly rape-y, hotly inflamed thwarted lovers was apparently as irresistible as the women themselves (and the narrative less able to defend itself). See, for example, Domne Eafe's oldest daughter, Mildburh, who somehow manages to seek refuge from courtship-by-abduction in the same Abbey that she was said to have founded. It's almost as if virginity isn't proper virginity if some sufficiently ardent man hasn't been beaten off with a stick — a woman's virtue is only valuable if it is under threat.

Still, there was something about the chaste woman that spoke into the physicality of women's existence. For most of history, women have been mostly about their bodies: having or not having sex, having or not having children, cleaning the dead bodies of their kin and attending to the bloody, sweating, gasping, wracked bodies of women in childbirth. Theirs have been bodies that have fed children from fluids of their own making, and their monthly bleeding, which

---

[1] Only after, you'll notice, having been eaten.

cannot be held and confined to the business of a closet like defecation can, forces physicality on them in the turning of each month. Time and time again sexist stereotypes describe women as being fundamentally more physical than men, more driven and controlled by their bodies, more subject to their passions. We saw in chapter 3 how, for centuries holiness in women and robust health were often held to be mutually exclusive, so antithetical are our bodies to godliness. Barton and Weil are both subject to crippling illness and most of our Kentish saints either die young like Eanswythe or have an extremely frail old age, like Mildthryth and Mildburh. Heaven overwhelms the physical — in women, at least.

Refusing marriage, sex and children, then, takes the woman's body into a strange asocial, unbiological, liminal place. It defies social convention while at the same time playing into its prejudices. It makes her almost otherworldly; it makes her *body* a token of that place where the saints *neither marry nor are given in marriage*. So, often, virgin martyrs' corpses are discovered incorrupt, as 'undefiled' by death as by men. Their bodies, in life and in death are already part of heaven. Edith, Mildthryth, Eadburh, again and again the coffins of virgin saints are opened and the bodies found to be as fresh as a daisy (and Edith's case, quite lively). The virgin saints speak of bodies converted to the business of heaven in a way that both undermined patriarchal determination but somehow at the same time confirmed it. It almost makes them men.

We see this, par excellence, in the story of **Mildthryth** (see, I told you I would get to her). Mildthryth ticks all the boxes for the early Anglo-Saxon saints: she is royal, educated, not just celibate but an abbess, and she is a 'proper' virgin, not just a chaste widow (*castitas*) or someone not having sex for fun but only for children (*iugalitas*), but a never-had-sex, intact hymen, *uirginitas* (which, frankly, sounds like a disease). She is also, to put the cherry on the top, the daughter of a saint.

Mildthryth is the middle daughter of Domne Eafe (she of the murdered nephews, miraculous deer et cetera). At a fairly young age Mildthryth is integrated into the network of educated Anglo-Saxon women by being sent to school in Gaul in a Frankish convent — Chelles.[2] There, by all accounts, she thrives. The stories describe her as generally well liked and identified as talented. A saint in the making.

Then comes the assault upon her dedication to celibacy. Enter, stage right, an eligible and powerful suitor; behold, stage left, local abbess who is either concerned to set Mildthryth up for a prosperous future, or a procuress, depending on the telling. As is proper in such stories, therefore, Mildthryth has no defence from the ardent suitor except her faith and her fleetfootedness. She makes a dash back to Kent. Fully convinced of her desire to be a bride of Christ, rather than of the aforementioned lusty aristocrat, the young Mildthryth takes the veil under Archbishop Theodore ("and 70 maidens with her"), somewhere in the region of 670AD. On the death of her mother, she takes over as abbess in Thanet.

Armed with a crozier and sacramental authority, Mildthryth proceeds to exercise peak abbess-itude. She has already demonstrated her capacity as a scholar whilst at Chelles, now she adds skills as a teacher, steward, worship leader and preacher. She positively glows with discipline and learning and wit. Oh, and charity: she is renowned for the assistance she gives to the poor surrounding the Minster. Her excellence, which was identified at school, is now confirmed by the whole region. Mildthryth is generally considered to be awesome.

When she dies, therefore, her successor, Eadburh (who is possibly, but not necessarily, the same Eadburh as at Lyminge, remember and, just possibly, also Mildthryth's great-aunt) immediately identifies her as a saint and builds a better church to house her in than the one where she initially rests. This is where we start to touch upon this theme of bodily sanctity: when Mildthryth's original tomb is opened in order to move her, the corpse is incorrupt and fragrant.

This self-evidently holy *body* then becomes the scoreboard for a rivalry between the abbeys of Saint Augustine's and Saint Gregory's — the former a monastery, the latter a house of secular canons —

---

[2] The one founded by Balthild, the incredibly-powerful-Frankish-Queen-Regent probably related to our Kentish Royals, that Chelles.

who start to behave like two dogs fighting over a bone (or in this case, 206 bones). In one account,[3] King Cnut gives the land of Minster at Thanet to St Augustine's. Cnut allegedly tells the monks that they need the permission of the women at Thanet to remove the sacred relic which is the mortal remains of Mildthryth. The sisters, understandably, refuse. The monks decide to take it anyway. Wonderfully, the monks stage a party at the Minster with — I'm assuming, I don't know — singing and dancing, because the party is supposed to cover the noise of the execution of the monks' plan, as well as focus the attention of the sisters in another direction. However, Eadburh has made Mildthryth's tomb so substantial that the noise of the monks breaking the tomb disturbs the party and the monks are rumbled. Being of stout heart, and much determined, the monks nevertheless gather up the remains of the dead abbess and leg it, pursued — as Shakespeare might have said — by nuns, back to Canterbury.

(There! Was the story not worth the wait?)

In the other account, told by Saint Gregory's, the Minster at Thanet is overwhelmed by Danish Vikings. The nuns, so the story goes, choose to be burnt to death rather than face violent gang rape at the hands of the Danes, but the tomb of Mildthryth is undamaged by the flames. The nuns then retreat to Lyminge, on account of the Viking attacks (no, I'm not sure how they managed to do this when they've been burned to death, either). Naturally, they take Mildthryth with them to re-inter in Lyminge with Eadburh (who may or may not already be at Lyminge). Eventually the buildings at Lyminge are also rendered uninhabitable. The lands pass into the hands of the archbishops of Canterbury and thence to St Gregory's, who take stewardship of their relics. This is why, when the canons at Saint Gregory's acquire the mortal remains of Eadburh, they get two for the price of one.

Both religious houses claim the inheritance of Mildthryth's corpse because *her very body* has been sanctified by the physicality of her commitment to Christ. (Although, granted, Saint Augustine's story is

---

[3] Told, unsurprisingly by the monks of St Augustine's Abbey

the more plausible.) In the game of my-house-is-holier-than-your-house, the bones of this dead virgin made a — literal — tangible difference. Of course, this tug-of-war ignores the sisters who are Mildthryth's community, but it is telling that in their own narrative, when the Thanet sisters moved to Lyminge — which we know they did — they also argue that they have Mildthryth's remains, as do the little remnant community in Canterbury. It is Mildthryth's actual body that gives them their identity and implied sanctity. Again in the cases of Edith, Eanswythe, Eadburh — their bodies are more than just corpses, they are icons of heaven. Because of the physical demonstration of their commitment to Christ, their bodies are found to be incorrupt, a place where heaven breaks through.

One last note on this — I hesitate to say seminal — virgin is her description by the 10/11th century chronicler known only by his initial, 'B'. He has skin in the game. He is also a secular cleric and he's been employed by Saint Gregory's to write the history of Eadburh. In order to explain Eadburh's cohabitation in death with Mildthryth he ends up backtracking a way. His description of Mildthryth is given through the eyes of his age, laced with the Church's relatively new emphasis on religious gender hierarchy and the cult of the Blessed Virgin Mary, which seems to be evolving in tandem with this increased emphasis on masculine holiness.

For starters, we have a sincere admiration of her skills, discipline and intellect combined with a basic assumption that these are essentially masculine traits. Rather than minimising them, B attributes them to her virginity. By rejecting the world, she becomes heavenly, perfect, and therefore, like the angels, un-biological and *masculine*. Indeed, he writes that, "chastity is called the sister of the angels in heaven." He is writing under the influence of Aldhelm's recently written book on virginity (who knew there was such a thing?) *De Uirginitate*, which is very clear that holiness belongs to the male world. A woman's only entrance to their holiness, therefore, is by turning her back on her sex and striving for an un-bodied, intellectual, masculine union with God. (Thus, it is also important to B to establish that Eadburh is — in slightly brain twisting logic — a local but never-married *maiden* and also, but sort of not, Ethelberh the royal widow and founder of Lyminge. It's complicated. I refer you to chapter 2.)

Mildthryth's (and Eadburh's) intellect becomes 'manly' as is Eadburh's heart. Their struggles are pushed firmly into the realm of the spiritual. B omits all panting men, replacing this challenge with otherworldly oppression. Devils and angels beset and assist (respectively) the spiritual struggles of the saints B describes. Hearth and home are replaced by a spiritual kingdom and a marital union with Christ (he uses Psalm 45[4] *a lot*).

In an oddly incestuous twist to this, Mildthryth, the Bride of Christ, is the image of Christ's Mother, as B identifies Mildthryth in particular with the Blessed Virgin Mary. This is typical of his time. From the 10th century, the Virgin Mary is rapidly becoming almost the sole icon for female spirituality. Thus in her role of abbess, Mildthryth becomes a virgin mother: the virgin mother of nuns. As well as emphasising her 'manly' intellect and discipline, B underlines her gentle pastoral care of the sisters in her Minster. Like her spiritual struggles, and her domestic allegiance, her motherhood becomes spiritual, dis-embodied. She is the spiritual mother of sisters in her care.

Mildthryth's story, and the telling of it, demonstrates an uneasy alliance of two strands of sanctification of women: totemisation of physicality plus dis-embodiment of their spirituality. Their bodies are (to the male writer) alien and uncontrollable, but brought into a semblance of masculinity by defying and redirecting their essential biological purpose (for men). You would think this would be deeply unattractive to most women: "Fancy internalising all the male discomfort with your body and becoming an asexual aesthete? No?" The ubiquitousness of it — both in the women acclaimed for it and in the thousands of women who quietly sign up for it over

---

[4] " Hear, O daughter, consider and incline your ear;
forget your people and your father's house,
and the king will desire your beauty. ..
...The princess is decked in her chamber with gold-woven robes;
in many-coloured robes she is led to the king;
behind her the virgins, her companions, follow.
With joy and gladness they are led along
as they enter the palace of the king." (Psalm 45. 10-15)

the centuries — tells a different story. This isn't just a small group of hard core zealots, this sacred virginity is practised by a sizable portion of the population.

The popularity of women's houses, and then, later, of the various more informal celibate lives that were lived by religious women, argues for its own value. It offered women a demonstration of the sanctification of their bodies in a path other than childbirth, with all the latter's risk, pain and likelihood of grief. Celibacy, with all the slightly fetish-y credibility that went with it, allowed women to be more than their biology, while still being rooted in that same sexuality. Like St Sepulchre's convent sitting between town and, well, not gown but cowl, all these women under vows play off against each other these tensions and fetishes of the war of the sexes, to find a place of meaning and worth at the crossroads. Like Joan Burghersh, lying for perpetuity on the threshold of the Undercroft, vowesses' liminality breaks the male hold on the boundaries of the sacred. All those stories of women beating off suitors, and literally (hagiography, remember) reshaping the elements in order to avoid marriage and/or rape, these stories are not just the silly outworking of a Church over obsessed by sex. The stories were a real encouragement to women, examples of women controlling their own sexuality and fertility, and making of their *whole* selves an offering to God. Think how popular Margaret of Antioch was. In the very earliest hagiographies the (male) tellers display a degree of scepticism not present in comparable legends about men[5], yet her story is still told and retold by women, for women. Note, too, how often these accounts describe women fleeing to women for protection, even to the point of near incoherence — see how Mildburh is both sheltered by and also founds the Abbey up in Shropshire (I will come to her, I promise).

Some of this will have flowed out of the pagan Anglo-Saxon cultic significance of women. There are signs among the grave goods of pagan sixth century women, that in the re-creation of civilisation after the Romans left, women carved an (albeit gender specific) religious role. (I know, I know — unidentified object "must have been religious", but nevertheless

---

[5] Looking at you, George and Denys.

archaeologists[6] are pretty confident of this.) With the arrival of Christianity in Kent, the Church will have done what it does best and integrated local cultic expectations into its own values and doctrine. Those virgin martyrs from the early centuries of Christianity entered Anglo-Saxon culture and created the cultural engine that was the minster of the seventh and eighth centuries. Virginity (defined quite broadly before the Carolingian reforms) becomes a radical demonstration of a new reality in which life was more than survival, appetites and genetic reproduction.

This new liberty enabled women to look beyond home and hearth — *Kinder, Küche, Kirche* — and beyond the social constraints of sex, to the call of heaven.

And since the call of heaven almost always sends us back into the world, so these women, as we saw in the first couple of chapters, were up to their elbows in the economic, social, educational as well as ecclesiastical world of their region. They were able to be, because they were virgins (/widows). Often and oftener, the women in this book have been, for one reason or another, freed from, or resistant to the demands of sexuality and domesticity in order to focus on social, political, religious or educational reform, on the poor or the vulnerable, on study — in short, on the things of God. Scholars and activists, ecclesiastical pioneers and patrons: most of them were free of both dependency and dependents. We marvel at the married women, like Fry and Gilmore,[7] who manage to extend themselves beyond their household. It is the unmarried women and the widows who are most available in terms of mental space, resources and time.

Often this is costly. Charlotte Boyd's single status contributed to her being buried in an unremarkable unmarked grave. Elizabeth Elstob, similarly, had no other safety net when her brother died. Elizabeth Carter fared better, but was nevertheless exasperated by the necessity of having constantly to fend off suitors. They were women who discomfited society by being resolutely single, but who enriched the Church

---

[6] The Canterbury Archaeological Trust, anyhow.
[7] Gilmore was a widow, yes, but eight nephews and nieces to care for, remember.

significantly because of it. This is worth remembering in a Church that still looks slightly askance at single people generally.

Some of the totemisation that we saw above had another interesting side effect. Let's take Mildthryth's older sister **Mildburh** (I said I would). She, like her sister, is born in the mid-7th century and educated in France; she, too, has an excessively ardent admirer. This is where the story starts to get a bit wibbly wobbly. Mildburh's romance takes place, without explanation, back in Shropshire. We don't know how or why she's there. (Mildburh, Mildthryth and Mildgyth were all brought up in the kingdom of Mercia, while their mother was still married to King Merewalh.) Mildburh's admirer is, so the story goes, a neighbouring prince whose courtship doesn't stop at letter writing. He decides that what Mildburh really needs to persuade her is a *surprise* romantic weekend away. Unconvinced, Mildburh flees through a storm only to find her path blocked by the river (I have some hope that the river in question might be the wonderfully named Shyte Brook but it's far more likely to be the Severn). Mildburh manages to cross the river, possibly with miraculous help, perhaps simply on the ford near Wenlock that was in use since forever until bridges got easy. Either way, the river then swells to un-crossable proportions[8]. Mildburh thereby gains enough time to seek shelter with the sisters at Wenlock, before founding the same Abbey with the help of her brother and father. Go figure. It is possible that there was some sort of nascent community there, which Mildburh formalised with her family connections and wealth. Maybe the community made a grab for the extra credibility of her name as a foundress, once Mildburh had been recognised locally as a saint. Maybe her family did give her the resources to found a community in Wenlock, but the necessity of the story, the need for her to find shelter in a Christian community, shaped the narrative. There's no way of knowing at this distance.

What is clear is that history is not the only thing that has shaped the narrative. While Wenlock's origins are old enough to be almost entirely obscured by the mists of time, there is a strong likelihood that the

---

[8] Possibly a reference to the Severn bore.

memory of Mildburh — a virgin with a powerful connection to the divine — collected trace elements of an earlier memory, or perhaps memories. The flooding river is reminiscent of the story of a local river goddess which involves similar tropes. Her miracles, too, smack of water/fertility goddess devices. As well as the usual healing miracles, there are stories of the sun holding up her slipped veil, or fire flowing out of her in the healing of a child and of the birds obeying her commands. Significantly, she was said to have a particular influence over barley, both protecting it and causing it to grow exceptionally well. Mildburh was also said to have made a spring form near Wenlock. The nature of the stories has led many commentators to suggest that Mildburh was used to replace an earlier worship of the local goddess. Given the shortage of specific goddesses connected to Wenlock, I think it more likely that she simply began to fulfil the function that was lost when the old gods were put aside.

Take Mildburh's great aunt, **Eanswythe**. Again, we know almost nothing about her except the stories wrapped around her memory. The very oldest histories tell us only her name, parentage, and the fact that she founded a Minster at Folkestone. From the stories, and from the other histories that we know, we can sketch out a little more.

Eanswythe is the daughter of Eadbald's second marriage, born shortly before the time of her father's death in 641 A.D. Eadbald himself is an interesting character. It looks as though he never wholeheartedly took his father, Ethelbert's, new faith, but his marriage to Ethelbert's second wife — whose name seems to have been totally expunged from the histories — was scandalous. Consequentially, it seems, (and, like Bertha's father) he became an apostate for the sake of the consanguineous marriage. His pagan rule totally upset the missionary apple cart and both Melitus, Bishop of London, and Justus, Bishop of Rochester, fled to Frankia. The Christian mission in Kent all but stopped. Then Eadbald married again, this time, it seems, to a good Christian woman totally unrelated to him before marriage. There is a fighting chance that it was international pressure that brought him back into the Christian fold, but it might have been another example of mission-by-marriage.

Either way, there is a boat at Sutton Hoo, said by some to be Eadbald's cenotaph (the Kingdom of Kent at this time stretched to the Humber) which, if his, suggests that his second conversion was no more wholehearted than his first. The boat is a pagan grave littered with Christian symbols. Bede records that Eadbald worshipped at two altars. Eadbald appears to be a man who liked to keep his options open.

Anyway, the third generation of Christian kings set out to do things differently. Eadbald's son, Eaconberht, is the first of his family to be a cradle Christian. It was Eaconberht who put in place legislation, for the first time, banning paganism in Kent. It is Eaconberht, rather than Eadbald, who is the principal family influence on Eanswythe. The chances are good that Eanswythe is sent to be educated at Balthild's minster at Chelles in the 640s, after her uncle has become the mayor of the palace of Neustria. Eanswythe is, in all events, an extremely well connected woman, a close relative of the King of Kent (his sister), near relative of the powerful Royal family across the channel (by her paternal grandmother) and possibly also related to the Regent Queen's right-hand man, Erchinoald (by her mother). As we've seen, Balthild is busy setting up a network of women's religious houses at which the aristocratic women of Europe will be educated for several centuries. Eanswythe comes out from, it seems, under Balthild's wing to found, most likely with her evangelistic brother's help, a minster at the bustling industrial hub at Folkestone. The minster is seeded with Roman monks and Frankish nuns, we're told. Eanswythe dies young. Probably.

Then we have the stories. As well as the usual array of healing miracles that we can expect from a saint of her vintage, there is a rather splendid story that involves the resurrection of a stolen goose that was not only cooked but eaten (as well as the reassurance of its slightly traumatised goosey brethren). There is also an ardent, slightly rape-y admirer, who looks suspiciously like her aunt's husband, causing several hagiographists to cry plagiarism. (He is a pagan prince of Northumbria who is culturally deaf to the whole 'no means no' thing until Eanswythe challenges him to a prayer-off. Whoever can persuade their god to extend the badly cut plank to fit in its proper place in the chapel gets to decide who marries whom. Needless to say the god that has done a stint at carpentry — and indeed, coincidentally, pulled off the same miracle himself as a child[9] — wins. Eanswythe's virginity survives the test of the panting male and all cry "Hurrah!") Finally, and this is the one I'm underlining, she causes water to *run uphill* for the sake of her new community. Eanswythe's holy body brings nearer the new Jerusalem where waters of life flow through the city. Just as in the heavenly city the conflicts between humans and the rest of nature are resolved, so the impact of this heavenly woman is beginning to mould the place to the people who live in it. The water retains her name centuries after her cult is evicted from the Priory.

Eanswythe's minster, one of the first stone buildings in the area since the Romans, would have dominated the landscape as well as (have I mentioned this?) the culture and economy of the area. It did not, however, survive as a double house. The minster is sufficiently protected by the cliffs and probable fortifications to survive the Danish attacks but in the 12th century it moves further inland *taking with it the remains of Eanswythe*. By the time Henry VIII is reaching out his fat fingers for the monastic harvest, the Priory at Folkestone is a small, limping affair. Nonetheless, the seal on the Acknowledgement of Supremacy (1534) is a picture of Eanswythe, holding a book and a crozier: the epitome of an Anglo-Saxon abbess. Folkestone Priory is stripped of its assets in 1535 and the ornamented reliquary of the greater part of her skull[10] disappears. At this point Eanswythe's body disappears (dang dang daaang!) Her influence, however, does not.[11]

In 1868 (around the time that Hill was beginning to get her teeth into charitable organisation, Boyd was setting up her orphanage and Hilda Stewart was settling into the religious life) Folkestone gets a new vicar. The Rev Matthew Woodward is an adherent of

---

[9] Not, I should add, according to the Gospels but according to popular Christian legend of the time
[10] No, I don't understand, either.
[11] I found this collect, date and source unknown:
O God, who has presented blessed Eanswythe to thy Church as one most worthy of honour, and bestowed her as a precious jewel on your heavenly citizens, render us, through her merits and prayers so pleasing to you in this life that we may be found worthy to share in the bliss to come, through our Lord Jesus Christ.

the now well established Oxford movement and turns his sights to the reorganisation of the chancel at St Mary and St Eanswythe's Church. In 1885, the workmen in the final stages of project Elevate the Altar find a small cavity, and inside the small cavity is a small casket, and inside the small casket is an ancient corpse.

The Rev Woodward is immediately convinced that his corpse is the mortal remains of Eanswythe. The 150-year controversy that follows (resolved in 2020 — spoiler: yes, it's Eanswythe) is important for the same reason that the brouhaha over Mildthryth and Eadburh is important in the 11th century. In the bodies of these women is the tangible remembrance of holiness, written in flesh dedicated to God; in the bodies of these women, held in a particular place, is a sense of the relationship between geography and the divine, between place and community and God.

For most of human history, we have depended on a sense of place and with that place we have woven stories about our relationship to the ground and the flora and fauna. There are whole libraries of sociological reflection on the roadside shrines that mark our modern, displaced need to make physical our history. These holy women whose bodies are a testament to their faith, and whose bodies sanctified the communities that came after them, made physical witness of a new reality, rooted in their community. They did something subtly different from the old local gods, because they offered a real promise of holiness. Unlike the old gods, theirs was a holiness you could imitate by the simple method of baptism and Christian discipline — and, for "hem that wolde lyve parfitly,"[12] abstention.

This is why you find stories of stone that holds Mildthryth's footprints, and festivals around the well at Kemsing dedicated to a woman who spent only a few short months in Kent. Their lives gave people a connection to creation and place through the worked example of their bodies. It is easy to see why the Reformers tore down every shred of this and ridiculed it. Theirs was a religion which had no truck for the

---

[12] As the wife of Bath said

instinctive or the irrational, but the loss of these local shrines did not reduce the need for connection.

Perhaps this is why the Protestant Reformation was so adamant that women should marry, and why Protestant societies have a tendency to belittle women that don't: because the memory of those holy virgin bodies was everything the Reformers hated. Very few of these holy virgins made it through Cranmer's purge of the calendar of saints in the 16th century. There is an irony to this, because the other side of the coin was the memory of women famous for their intellectual and spiritual focus, a focus which is at the heart of the Protestant ideal. Moreover, this focus is much harder for women who are also juggling obligations to family and hearth in societies where domestic labour is theirs, or their responsibility. By this reckoning, the Protestant eradication of the religious vocation hamstrung in women the very spirituality it sought to cultivate.

Sadly, all that remains of this spirituality of physical abstention is the bit that suits patriarchal culture: the emphasis on women's virginal *purity* (until such time as they marry and start producing children). Many feminists have pointed out the toxic quality of this model; popular culture laughs at its prudishness. What both groups have missed is the powerful message of celibacy, which liberates both men and women from the dominion of appetite and biology. To revive the celebration of the likes of Eanswythe, Mildthryth and Edith is to give women a model of faith by which their bodies are a witness to a different reality. These lives, like those of so many subsequent virgins (in the wider, Old English sense), like Boyd, Gilmore, Carter and Hilda, are redirected to the service of the community, to the glory of God. These lives, in intentional abstention from appetite and the biological imperative to reproduce, are a demonstration — to deploy a rather tired cliché — of human *being* rather than human *doing*. This vision is one, too, which subverts the hierarchy of the sexes, described in Genesis 3 as a feature of our fall from grace. It rebukes the male gaze and reclaims our sexuality. It is also a model which resonates with the paradoxes of Christianity: in the tension between the flesh and spirit, the transcendent and the imminent, the tensions inherent in the incarnate God.

Virginity is not just about an absence of sex, nor even, really, about penis-related taint. In fact, both historically and today, we are distracted by all this language of purity from the truth to which virginity seeks to witness. Virginity is the consecration of the flesh to the eternal reality: a demonstration of the *this-worldly* resurrection of the body and the transformation of biology to the work of heaven. It is a rejection of the eternal life of biological reproduction, for a life lived as in heaven, where *they neither marry nor are given in marriage.*[13] The nuns are not insipid women, fleeing the everyday realities of life, they are vibrant with the resonances of heaven, revealing the transformation of creation itself.

Did I not say you'd be surprised what a nun can do?

---

[13] Mark 12:25 (NRSV)

Conclusion

In 1852 Florence Nightingale wrote to the Dean of Westminster, Arthur Stanley,

> *"For women [the Church of England] has — what?... I would have given her my head, my hand, my heart. She would not have them. She did not know what to do with them."*

I am not the first to remark that the Church is striking by its lack of female-specific roles. Nearly everything women do in and for the Church is carved out of masculine identities and masculine patterns of holiness. We need women to counterweight the male narrative. We also need women simply to be women so that the richness and variety of God's tapestry might be displayed in all its beauty, so that the wide range of what this means can be imagined and appreciated by the whole community. Too often excluded, far fewer of us can contribute as the women of this book have, and the kingdom of God is the poorer for it.

That seminal companion to the calendar of saints, *Exciting Holiness*, describes saints as "those heroes of the faith whose lives have excited others to holiness." Certainly the capacity for women's witness to encourage other women is demonstrated again and again in the pages of this book and acknowledged by the likes of John Foxe. Joan Bocher's long imprisonment, when she consistently defended her ideas and held her ground against the might of the Church, gave "no small encouragement to others," noted the 17th century chronicler, Peter Heylyn. I hope that there have been women in this book who have encouraged you. It's impossible to cover everything, but herein we've seen wives and virgins, aristocrats and more humbly born women, outgoing and shy.

Some have been more obviously 'holy' than others, some more evidently 'exciting', but all are women who have lived in response to the gospel that they have received. Many of them have done their best to hold out a helping hand to those coming behind them.

None of them were acting on their own, but are surrounded by family and friends, institutions and occasionally systems which have helped them witness, as Fry would have it, to the light within. Sometimes this has made the difference between life and death, poverty and affluence. Fry's family were a buffer between her husband's financial collapse and homelessness; both Elstob and Hill had no such buffer. While Hill had the benefit of a remarkable mother who forged a new life for the pair of them, Elstob was an orphan and the death of her brother was the death of her career. Ethelberh picked up the torch carried by Mildthryth before her and Ethelburga (assuming she's a different person) benefited by the missionary team that travelled with her to Northumbria. Gilmore learned her nursing in the style brought to England by Fry. This is how it is for us all. No one is an island, as the poet said. Most of us need a leg up at some point. Each one of us has a role not only witnessing to our own light, but also allowing our brothers and sisters in Christ to demonstrate the face of God in them.

However, it's been noticed by others that, "behaviour which was held to imply sanctity in men only appeared as insanity when engaged in by women" (Richard Symonds, Society of Friends). Consistently we have seen objections to women having an education/conscience/vocation independent of their husband/father/priest. Sometimes, these objections have resulted in systematic pushback. What is achieved by one generation can be undone in another, and has been, repeatedly. While I derived tremendous encouragement from the stories I found, I also saw a stark warning. The ministry and vocation of women to be and do as God is calling them has been repeatedly restrained, often under the adjective of 'reform'. The 20th century Church was not first to give women access to the pulpit and the font, and if we are not careful it will not be the last to think that it is innovating in doing so. The stories in this book are above all else a reminder to ensure that we continue to look behind us to make sure that the door stays open and free.

This would be easier if there were more visible women in the celebrations of the Church. Time and again in the writing of this work I have seen a stark contrast between the celebrations of the contributions by men to the glory of God and those by women. We need more women in our calendar of saints and in our liturgy. Where is the poetry of women alongside the canticles by men? Where is the hymnody by women? Where is the imagery celebrating the feminine within the Godhead? When the words on our lips and imaginations of our hearts include the witness of women as much as men we will see a more complete picture of the glory and nature of God.

This work has also been an education in the beauty to be found in the stories of the women who have simply got on with being the person that they are. They haven't innovated or reformed anything, but they have been a sign to the people around them of the love of God. Often this is with their bodies, whether in conscious virginity or in motherhood and the God-given enjoyment of their "things smale". There have been women between these pages, too, whose bodies have seemed antithetical to their vocation or well-being. There are women like Barton, whose experience of the divine has almost seemed to break their bodies, and others like Weil and Carter who have felt their bodies to be an inconvenience and a distraction. This does not, I think, undermine the significance of our be-souled bodies, but serves to underline that there is no getting away from them. Our bodies are, more than anything, what we hold in common with each other and with our God. There is no secret 'me' hidden under the guise of my body, any more than there is a true 'me,' if only I could get away from all the pesky people who keep distracting me.

This tension between the inner and the outer 'me,' between the social and the private 'me,' is a tension often demonstrated in the lives of women in particular. Our bodies are public property[1] but our

---

[1] Doubt me? Then take a look at how hard a woman has to prove that she has *demonstrated* the refusal of her body to another man, how a pregnant woman's behaviour is fair game for comment, how any woman's body is fair game for personal comment by any stranger.

voices are kept out of the public square, our private selves are so often sunk into the identities and activities of the people around them[2]. Women are often liminal, existing across the boundaries of public and private, physical and spiritual: the majority sex that exists on the fringe of human identity. Perhaps, perhaps this is why women are so much more likely to populate the congregations of our churches. Holiness is also inherently liminal, connecting the mundane to the divine, and, in this, women are already halfway there, in their understanding and experience of their own lives.

Eanswythe founded one of the first communities of women in Kent and had an active, if short, ministry caring for the people in her community, but her 'afterlife' in the imagination of the people of Folkestone wove her into the life of the spirit of the place. Anne Boleyn might be counted among the Reformation martyrs, but she was also for a time a successful politician and patron using her wealth and authority to change the life of the nation as well as improving the lives of individuals. Hilda Stewart OSB had the care of a community of women, but she was also part of a movement that was reimagining how women might respond to the Gospel. Few of us, if any, have only one face but if our stories are only ever told from the outside they are usually flat, one-dimensional affairs.

I suspect this is why many of the roles in this book that are distinctively female are also distinctively liminal: the prophetess,[3] the virgin mother[4] and the strange way in which women translate into *genii locorum*.[5] This last, when saints pass into folklore, welded into the character and well-being of that place,

---

[2] The most obvious example is the way most women lose their family names on marriage, and then the experience of many new mothers is the loss of their given name for the first few years of the child's life, becoming instead "[Name of Child]'s Mummy".
[3] I say that the role of prophetess is distinctly female not because men are not prophetic, as much as that the *role* of prophetess, as a subversive feature of Western Christian history, has had no real male parallel. By and large men are either inside politics seeking reform or rebels, while women have been allowed a strange, if dangerous, respect when they have spoken truth to power as a proxy for the voice of God.
[4] Similarly, men have run celibate communities but this role has not been construed with as much cultic resonance as when a virgin takes on a maternal office.
[5] Plural of *genius loci,* the presiding god or spirit of a place.

is perhaps the apotheosis of feminine liminality. I am inclined to conclude that it is also why the holiness of women is often interpreted as transgressive, when it is about escaping from — existing across — the boundaries (a.k.a. pigeonholes). The multifacetedness, which is expected by men of men, becomes discomforting in women when they inhabit several spaces.

In short, the holiness of women reflects the holiness of all of us, in its complexity and ambiguity; it reflects aspects of God unrevealed if our stories aren't told. Some of us are brighter lights, or more distinctive flowers, than others, but all of us serve the beauty of the Kingdom. Anyone might be someone's 'first' — doctor, licensed reader, neighbour, human — but we exist in a great cloud of witnesses. I'm hoping this book has served to amplify the cheers of some of those witnesses, women whose wholehearted 'yes' to God has been played out in a great variety of ways.

And what more should I say? For time would fail me to tell of Aette, Wilnotha, Mary More, Osyth Lucie-Smith, Elizabeth Hull and their sisters who, through faith, transformed kingdoms, administered justice, obtained promises, lost their homes, built communities, faced the edge of the sword, won strength out of weakness, faced down kings, put foreign gods to flight.

All of them are the spiritual daughters of that Christian woman[6] who, if not the first in Kent, then the one who crucially opened the door to their wider Christian witness in minsters, parishes, town squares and all the many facets of life in Kent. All these women contributed to the history of the Church in this county. Now it is our turn.

---

[6] (Bertha, I mean.)

Thanksgiving for the (Kentish) Holy Ones of God (of Kent)[1]

For Bertha and Ethelburh, ambassadors for the faith,
and for all who use their networks for mission;
For Saexburh and Avicia, abbesses,
and for all who lead communities of witness;
For Sarah Forbes Bonetta and all who,
> with courage and conviction
carried the gospel into strange lands.

For Eadburh, and all who command authority
to nurture and teach the children of God;
For Joan Bauford and Susan May,
> and all who are determined to speak
and preach the Word of God;
For Hilda Stewart and Isabella Gilmore,
and for all who find new patterns
> for existing forms of service.

For Elizabeth Barton, prophetess,
and all who call us to holiness,
> and speak truth to power;
For Joan Bocher, and for all who,
> with boldness and persistence
contend for the truth of the gospel;
For Elizabeth Rede, and all the nuns of Kent
who held fast to their vows as Brides of Christ.

For Anne Boleyn, Queen and martyr,
and for all who serve their country with integrity;
For Eleanor Plantagenet, and all who strive
to bring to birth their vision for the land.

For Countess Goda and Joan Burghersh, patrons,
and all whose giving equips the Church of God;

---

[1] Based on on "Thanksgiving for the Holy Ones of God" in *Common Worship: Christian Initiation*.

For Marjorie Sands, and all who give
quietly, steadily, enabling the service of others.

For Pocahontas, serving a people not her own
and all who create bridges between worlds;
For Domne Eafe and Wulfthryth, peacemakers,
and all who shine as lights in the darkness.

For Edith of Kemsing, artist and scholar
and all who delight in the Book of Creation;
For Elizabeth Elstob and Elizabeth Carter
and for all who share the light of Wisdom;
For Simone Weil, philosopher,
and for all who yearn for justice and truth.

For Octavia Hill and Elizabeth Fry
and for all who work to transform the world.

For Joan of Kent and Matilda of Boulogne,
and for those whose devotion to family
       allows others to flourish;
For Margaret Roper, scholar and advocate,
and those who risk everything for kith and kin.

For Mildthryth, Mildburh and Eanswythe, holy virgins,
and all who worship God
       with everything they have and are.

For all the unsung heroes of our faith,
whose names are known to God alone:

For all those in our own lives
who have brought us to this time and place
and shown to us the way of holiness:

Let us praise them with thankful hearts:
and glorify our God in whom they put their trust.

A timeline

FOURTH CENTURY

313
Latest possible date for the martyrdom of Alban because in

314
Christianity becomes legal in the Roman Empire.

314
Bishop Restitutus, probably from Londinium (London), is one of the British delegation who attends the church synod or Council held at Arelate (Arles), in Gaul, demonstrating an ecclesiastical infrastructure in Southeast England.

FIFTH CENTURY

410
Britain asks the Roman emperor Honorius for help against increased incursions from the Saxons, Scots, Picts and Angles. He writes back telling them to 'look to their own defenses.' No help is forthcoming. This letter is usually considered to mark the end of Roman Britain.

431
Pelagius, a British monk, is declared a heretic by the Council of Ephesus.

480
Benedict of Nursia is born. He will go on to write his Rule for monastic communities.

496
King Clovis of the Franks is baptised

SIXTH CENTURY

During the sixth century, a cemetery is established on Dover Hill, overlooking the site of the now ruined Roman villa above East Wear Bay. The items found with the men, women and children buried here reflected the material culture of east Kent at the time, including Kentish products displaying a fusion of southern Scandinavian and Frankish material culture, as well as Frankish imports, and items from further afield, including by the seventh-century Amethyst beads from Persia, and beads made from an Egyptian cowrie shell, indicating that the community here is able to tap into Kent's maritime trading relationships.

Circa 580
Bertha, daughter of King Charibert of Paris, marries Æthelberht, the son of King Eormenric. Bertha, a Christian, is then accompanied to Kent by a Frankish bishop, Luidhard.

597
St Augustine arrives in Kent. By this date Æthelberht has succeeded his father as King of Kent. Æthelberht receives Augustine and directs him to establish his mission at Canterbury, where Bertha and Luidhard already used the Church of St Martin for worship.

SEVENTH CENTURY

601
Æthelberht is baptised by this date. Canterbury Cathedral is founded by Augustine a year later.

604
Rochester Cathedral is founded, likewise by Augustine.

c. 610
Bertha dies, and Æthelberht re-marries, although the name of his second wife is not recorded.

616/18
On 24th of February (in either 616 or 18) King Æthelberht dies and is succeeded by his son Eadbald. Eadbald takes his stepmother as his wife, causing a rift with the Christian Church. Mellitus, Bishop of London, and Justus, Bishop of Rochester, leave Kent for Francia in response.

624
King Eadbald converts to Christianity (again?). In order to have been accepted by the Church, Eadbald must by this time have set aside his first wife (and stepmother). Subsequently, he married Imme (Emma), a Frankish Christian, possibly a close relative of Erchinoald who later became mayor of the palace of Neustria (Northern France, in today's geography).

Later in the year, Edwin, king of Northumbria, agrees to the marriage terms for Eadbald's sister Æthelburga, which include that she be allowed to practise the Christian faith. Æthelburga travels north, accompanied by Bishop Paulinus (who later becomes Bishop of Rochester after fleeing Mercia).

Mid-620s to late 630s
Within this period the three known children of Eadbald and Imme, their sons Eorcenbert and Eormenred and their daughter Eanswythe are born. Radiocarbon dating of relics at Folkestone suggest that Eanswythe is likely to have been born sometime after 635, rather than earlier.

c. 633
Edwin's death at the Battle of Hatfield Chase. Æthelburga returns to Kent. Possible foundation of Lyminge Abbey

640
King Eadbald dies, on 20th January according to Frankish annals, and is succeeded by his son Eoreonbert. Some sources claim that Eormenred died before his father Eadbald, others that initially both sons ruled as joint kings.

641
Erchinoald succeeds Aega as the mayor of the palace of Neustria, making him the power behind the Frankish throne. If he is related to Imme, then he would also be a close relative and powerful potential ally of king Eorcenbert, Bertha's grandson and Eanswyth's brother.

c. 650
Erchinoald gives his slave Balthild, said to have been of Saxon (perhaps Anglo-Saxon) birth, to the young King Clovis II. Clovis II subsequently marries her and the couple have three sons.

Sometime in this decade Domne Eafe, Eormenred's daughter, marries Merewalh of Mercia, having three daughters (Mildthryth, Mildburh and Mildgytha) and a son (Merefin) by him.

Also in the 650's or, at the very latest, in 660, Eanswythe likely dies, aged 17-20. The timing of the foundation of a minster at Folkestone is uncertain, but falls around the same period, either posthumously, in honour of Eanswythe, or with her as its first abbess.

657/8-660
Queen Balthild rules as regent for her young son Chlothar III. One of her first acts is the foundation of a nunnery at the royal ville of Chelles, and she also establishes links with the existing nunneries at Jouarre and Faremoutiers-en-Brie. She goes on to promote the role of royal women in nunneries in both Francia and the Anglo-Saxon kingdoms, aided by Bertila, Abbess of Chelles, who may be a relative of Queen Bertha of Kent.

Merewalh of Mercia converts to Christianity.

664
Death of King Eorcenbert and Archbishop Deusdedit during an outbreak of plague. Eorcenbert is succeeded by his son Egbert I. During his reign his cousins Æthelred and Æthelbert are said to have been murdered in the royal villa at Eastry. This reign may also see the foundation of Minster-in-Sheppey by Eorcenbert's widow Seaxburh, possibly whilst she is acting as regent.

670s

This decade probably sees the death of Merewalh of Mercia and the return to Kent of Domne Eafe (Æbbe). The nunnery at Minster-in-Thanet is founded for her on the back of the murder of her brothers, Egbert's cousins, Æthelred and Æthelbert.

676
King Æthelred of Mercia invades Kent, destroying and plundering Rochester.

c. 694
Mildthryth becomes abbess of Minster-at-Thanet.

699

At Cilling, near Faversham, King Wihtred issues a confirmation of privileges to the churches and monasteries of Kent. The grant is made in the presence of four abbesses; Eormenhild, abbess of Minster-in-Sheppey, Æbbe, abbess of Minster-in-Thanet, Eormenburh, probably Abbess of Lyminge, and Nerienda, believed to be abbess of Folkestone.

EIGHTH CENTURY

Archaeological and documentary evidence suggests that the Kentish minsters flourish as centres of power and wealth during this century, as part of a vibrant network of trade spanning the North Sea and Channel. Because of their wealth, control of them becomes hotly contested between the competing royal dynasties of Kent, Mercia and Wessex, as well as between different factions within the Kentish Church.

c. 730
Mildthryth dies.

Eadburh is by now abbess at Thanet. She builds a new church and translates Mildthryth's remains into a new shrine therein.

762
Sigeburh is recorded as abbess at Thanet, followed by Selethryth towards the end of the century. During this time the abbey secures significant tolling privileges. Selethryth is known to be abbess of Lyminge also.

NINTH CENTURY

800
Charlemagne is crowned the first Holy Roman Emperor and begins a programme of extensive reforms of both Church and civic society.

804
Around this time, the community at Lyminge is given a retreat in Canterbury from the Danes. There's a possibility this might have been the seed community for St Sepulchre's.

833-9
Abba, a reeve in Kent, grants property to the convent of Folkestone, on condition that he be buried there and that his widow, Heregyth, be given the option of entering the community.

850
No longer any trace of the Lyminge community.

TENTH CENTURY

930s
Wulfthryth is born sometime this decade.

c. 950-974
The earliest extant document known as the 'Kentish Royal Legend', or sometimes as the 'Mildrith Legend', is written at some point during these years. It briefly mentions Eanswythe, stating that she was the daughter of King Eadbald and Ymme, and that she "...rests at Folkestone". The core text of the surviving version, which deals with the murder of the Kentish princes Æthelred and Æthelbert at Eastry in the seventh century, and the subsequent foundation of Minster-in-Thanet for their sister, Domne Eafe, may have been written down as early as the eighth- or ninth-centuries.

959
Edgar becomes King of Wessex after the sudden, *mysterious* death of his brother Eadwig.

Between 961 and 964
Edgar's first wife, Æthelflæd, dies; he 'marries' Wulfthryth; Wulfthryth gives birth to Edith at Kemsing; Edgar and Wulfthryth separate; Wulfthryth and Edith head to Wilton; Edgar marries Ælfthryth.

984-ish
Edith of Wilton dies.

991
The Anglo-Saxon Chronicle records that "In this year Olaf [Tryggvason, later king of Norway] came with 93 ships to Folkestone, and ravaged round about it...".

LATE TENTH- TO ELEVENTH CENTURIES

The 'Lives of the Kentish Royal Saints', a series of accretions to the Kentish Royal Legend, is probably written between 974 and 1030, fragments of which survive in two eleventh-century copies. One version, the Liber Vitae of Hyde Abbey (also referred to as Ða halgan) is produced in 1031.

This is also the period when the Old English Hexateuch is produced in Canterbury under the direction of Ælfric, Abbot of Eynsham. In all probability much of the illustrative work is done by women, possibly the sisters of Saint Sepulchre's Abbey.

1000
Wulfthryth dies.

c. 1004
Emma of Normandy, wife of King Ethelred the Unready, gives birth to Goda, later Countess of Vexin then of Boulogne.

1030s
By this decade Mildthryth's remains have been removed to Canterbury leaving the minster in Thanet poorer and weaker, such that the records are inconsistent in their reports of the community's continued existence.

1040s
Goscelin of Canterbury is born sometime in the 1040s. He takes religious vows early in life and by the 1060s is in England, collecting material for his hagiographies.

1042
Edward the Confessor crowned King of England.

Between 1047 and 1056
Countess Goda dies.

1063
Goda's son, Gautier, and his wife Biota, die *unexpectedly* while held prisoner by William, Duke of Normandy. Gautier was a favourite of the childless King Edward.

1066
Death of Edward the Confessor, succeeded (briefly) by Harold Godwinson. William of Normandy defeats King Harold Godwinsson at the Battle of Hastings.

1085
William I commissions the Domesday book, which records a small community of nuns holding 4 acres of land in Canterbury belonging to St Augustine's Abbey. This community will become Saint Sepulchre's Abbey.

1087
William II (Rufus) becomes King of England. During his reign he is known to have 'confirmed' Goda's grant of lands to Rochester Cathedral, and likely her Book of the Gospels.

c. 1090
Malling Abbey is founded by Bishop Gundulf of Rochester. Avicia remains prioress until Gundulf is on his deathbed, when she is given an Abbess' staff and swears obedience to Gundulf's successors.

TWELFTH CENTURY

1103
Matilda of Boulogne is born the daughter of Mary of Scotland and Eustace III of Boulogne.

1125
Matilda of Boulogne marries Stephen de Bois, the nephew of Henry I.

1130/33
Fire damages the new cathedral at Rochester. Further fires damage the cathedral 1137 and 1179.

1135
Henry I dies. Stephen is crowned king in London on Saint Stephen's day. His wife, Matilda, is crowned Queen the following Easter.

1136-8
With the assent and authority of John, Bishop of Rochester, the monks of Folkestone priory move to a new church and site outside the castle that had been gifted to them by William d'Avranches.

Eanswythe's remains are translated from the old church to the new.

1138

Maud, Countess of Anjou and rival for the throne of England sends troops to England under the command of Robert, Earl of Gloucester, her half-brother. The period of Civil War known as 'The Anarchy' begins.

1147

Matilda and Stephen found Faversham Abbey in thanksgiving for the peace accord, and Maud's retreat from England. Around this time, their daughter, Marie, becomes a novice at Higham.

1152

Matilda of Boulogne dies after a short fever. King Stephen is grief-stricken. Matilda is buried in Faversham Abbey.

1154

Stephen dies, being buried in Faversham with Matilda. Maud's son, Henry, takes the throne, the second king of his name.

1160

Marie of Boulogne, Abbess of Romsey (daughter to Matilda and Stephen) is kidnapped by Matthew of Alsace and held for 10 years before she can negotiate her return to the conventual life, at St. Austrebert, in Montreuil.

1170

Thomas Becket is murdered in Canterbury Cathedral.

THIRTEENTH CENTURY

1201

William of Perth is murdered in Rochester by his adopted son. He is subsequently declared a saint on account of a post-mortem healing of a passing woman. His cult in Kent for a time rivals that of Thomas Becket.

1215

Rochester Castle is besieged in the first Barons' War.

1216
King John, fourth child of Henry II, dies, to be succeeded by Henry III.

King John's widow, Isabella of Angoulême, returns to her family in France leaving her infant daughter, Eleanor, Countess of Pembroke, to be brought up by Peter des Roches, Bishop of Winchester (a.k.a. the Butterfly Bishop on account of a rather splendid Arthurian legend).

1224
Eleanor Plantagenet is married for the first time, to William Marshal, the son of that William Marshal who won the First Barons' Revolt for Eleanor's brother, Henry III.

1231
Eleanor Plantagenet is widowed for the first time. She subsequently swears an oath of chastity in the presence of Edmund Rich, Archbishop of Canterbury.

1238
Eleanor Plantagenet is married for the second time, to Simon de Montfort, who is in line to be the 6th Earl of Leicester. They go on to have seven children together.

1240
The main body of Rochester Cathedral is largely completed.

Sometime between 1240 and 1322
An extensive mural is painted on the wall of the south transept of Rochester Cathedral, depicting an unknown woman in prayer, surrounded by angels and female saints.

1256
Rome acknowledges the cult of William of Perth. Although there is no papal bill canonising him, Bishop John Sheppey appears to have visited Rome to ask for Pope Alexander IV to acknowledge the status quo.

1264
Second Barons' War. Earl Simon de Montfort and co. lay siege to Rochester Castle, causing havoc in the Cathedral. In the castle, the king's hall and other bailey buildings are burned. The castle eventually falls after the barons win the battle of Lewes, capturing the King. Simon de Montfort is brutally and shockingly

assassinated the following year, on the field of battle in Evesham. After his death, his wife, Eleanor Plantagenet, holds Dover Castle against Henry III's son, Edward, surrendering it later the same year.

1275
Eleanor Plantagenet dies at Montargis Abbey, a nunnery founded by Simon de Montfort's sister, Amicia.

FOURTEENTH CENTURY

1327
Edward III becomes king on the death of his father, Edward II.

1328
Joan of Kent is born, the daughter of Edmund, first Earl of Kent, grandson of Edward I.

1337
The start of the Hundred Years' War between the royal houses of England and France. The conflict continues to 1453 (126 years).

1340
Joan of Kent runs off with and marries Thomas Holland, somewhat informally. The following year her family marry her to William Montague, Earl of Salisbury.

Joan Burghersh is born around this time.

1349
A papal bull declares Joan of Kent's marriage to William Montague null and void.

c. 1360
John of Tynemouth writes his Sanctilogium, which includes a version of the *Life of St Eanswythe*. This almost certainly drew off an earlier, lost *Vita* of the Saint, perhaps of twelfth to thirteenth-century date. It includes the earliest known reference to her miracle of making water run up hill to supply her minster, thus indicating that St Eanswythe's watercourse (later known as the Town Ditch) is in existence by this date, is regarded as ancient, and is associated in legend with Eanswythe's cult.

Joan of Kent is widowed for the first time in 1360 and marries the son of Edward III, Edward Woodstock (the Black Prince), the following year.

1367
Edward, the Black Prince, becomes mortally ill.

1375
Joan Burghersh is widowed. The following year Joan of Kent is also widowed upon the death of Edward Woodstock.

1377
Joan of Kent's second son, Richard, grandson of Edward III, becomes king at the age of 10 (the second of his name).

1381
The Peasants' Revolt. Joan of Kent is escorted through the rebels to her son in the Tower of London. Richard's quelling of the rebellion is effective but brutal. Joan of Kent retreats from the Royal Court the following year.

1385
Joan of Kent dies, purportedly of a broken heart.

1399
Henry IV (also grandson of Edward III) of Lancaster deposes Richard II and takes the crown.

Joan Burghersh's tomb is completed, close to that of the Black Prince.

Geoffrey Chaucer's *Canterbury Tales* is written by now.

FIFTEENTH CENTURY

1404
Joan Burghersh dies and is the first woman to be buried in Canterbury Cathedral.

1465/6
The will of Alice Jacob, dated 10th March, gives 4d to the Light of St Eanswythe.

c. 1490
Joan Bocher is born, Joan Knell, in Steeple Bumstead in Essex.

SIXTEENTH CENTURY

1505
Margaret Roper is born, Margaret More, in London, the daughter of Sir Thomas More and Jane Colt.

1509
Henry Tudor dies and is succeeded by Henry VIII as King of England. Sometime in this decade, Anne Boleyn is born in — and I'm emphatic about this — Hever Castle.

1521
Higham Abbey is the first of the Kentish convents to be dissolved.

Margaret More marries William Roper in Eltham, Kent.

1522
Margery Sandes leaves a number of goods as well as an annuity of 20½ shillings a year to the sisters at Malling Abbey.

1524
Margaret Roper completes a translation of Erasmus' treatise on the Lord's Prayer. It's the first published translation into English by a non-royal woman.

1525
Elizabeth Barton develops epileptic symptoms, alongside prophetic visions. In the following year she has a vision of the Virgin Mary resulting in the setting up of the shrine at Court-at-Street and Barton taking vows at St Sepulchre's Abbey, Canterbury.

1528
Joan Bocher is widowed and also arrested for the first time.

1532–1535
Anabaptists attempt to establish a theocracy at Munster, in what is now Germany. It doesn't end well, and is for decades afterwards — if not centuries — the principal cautionary tale against Anabaptists.

1532
Anne Boleyn becomes pregnant. Henry VIII makes her Marquess of Pembroke, giving her significant authority in her own right. The pair are married, and Anne Boleyn is crowned, the following year.

1534
Elizabeth Barton is arrested for treason and hung, drawn and quartered, with her head put on a spike at London Bridge.

Act of Succession is passed, declaring Anne Boleyn's daughter, Elizabeth Tudor, the next in line to the throne. The Act also declares Henry VIII Governor of the Church of England. It creates an Oath of Supremacy recognising the Act. Failure to swear this oath is declared to be treason. Sir Thomas More refuses and is consequently arrested.

1535
Following a visitation in October, Richard Layton, an agent of Thomas Cromwell, writes an unfavourable report on Folkestone Priory. He records that there is only the prior and one elderly monk and that "The house was in utter decay. It consisted of one hall, one chamber, a kitchen, and a little parlour underground, not meet for a monk; the barns were filled with corn, and there were a few cattle, but no household staff. The prior and the monk were both guilty of serious offences". Folkestone priory was surrendered to the crown on 15th November.

Thomas Cromwell appoints Margaret Vernon to run Malling Abbey, on Elizabeth Rede's resignation as Abbess.

Sir Thomas More is executed as a traitor. Margaret Roper retrieves his head from London Bridge before it is thrown into the Thames.

1536
Anne Boleyn is arrested and executed.

1538
The nuns of Malling Abbey refuse to sign the Deed of Surrender, but the abbey nevertheless passes into private ownership.

1543
Joan Bocher is arrested for the second time, in Frittenden in Kent.

1544
Margaret Roper dies, aged 39. She's initially buried in Chelsea, but is later interred in the Roper family vault

in Saint Dunstan's, Canterbury, along with her husband, and her father's head.

1546
Ann Askew is burnt at the stake for believing that Holy Communion is "a peece of bread".

1547
Henry VIII dies and is succeeded by his son Edward VI.

1549
Joan Bocher is arrested for the third time.

1550
Joan Bocher is burnt as a heretic, one of only two such deaths in Edward's reign, and the only woman.

1553
Edward VI dies. His cousin, Jane Gray is very briefly Queen, to be overthrown by Edward's sister, Mary.

Last recorded trace of the erstwhile sisters of Malling Abbey.

1554
The first edition of Foxe's Book of Martyrs (*Actes and monuments of these latter and perillous dayes, touching matters of the Church, wherein ar comprehended and described the great persecutions horrible troubles, that have bene wrought and practised by the Romishe prelates, speciallye in this Realme of England and Scotlande, from the yeare of our Lorde, a thousande, unto the tyme nowe present. Gathered and collected according to the true copies*) is published in Latin. The first edition in English is published in 1563. There are 13 more editions published over the next 300 years.

1555
Margery Polley is burnt as a heretic alongside Nicholas Wade. She is the first woman to die thus in Mary's reign.

1556
Joan Beach of Tonbridge is arrested with John Harpole and burnt at the stake in Rochester.

1558
Anne Albright, Joan Catmer, Joan Sole, and Agnes Snoth (Smith), are martyred in Canterbury.

SEVENTEENTH CENTURY

1603
James Stuart succeeds Elizabeth I as King of England.

1605
Guy Fawkes fails to blow up Parliament.

1608
Pocahontas meets John Smith. She's between 10 and 13 years old.

1613
Pocahontas is kidnapped by the English and is later baptised, taking the name Rebecca. She marries John Rolfe the following year.

1616
Pocahontas gives birth to Thomas Rolfe. She travels to London and visits the Royal Court, treated like a foreign Princess. She dies the following year, on her way to the port at Gravesend.

1641
A Discoverie of Six Women Preachers is published.

1642
Outbreak of the series of conflicts collectively known as the English Civil War.

1649
Execution of King Charles I. The Kingdom of England becomes the Commonwealth of England.

c. 1650
A stone coffin thought to be Eanswythe is found in the north wall of the south aisle of the Church of St Mary & St Eanswythe, Folkestone "...the corpse was found lying in its perfect form, and by it on each side an hour glass and several medals, the letters on which were obliterated, and several locks of her hair which were taken away and kept by different persons for the sanctity of it".

1660
Fall of the Commonwealth. Charles Stuart returns to England from exile (spending his first night in England at Restoration House in Rochester).

1683
Elizabeth Elstob is born

1685
James II of England takes the throne.

1689
Elizabeth Elstob is orphaned and moves to live in Canterbury with her uncle Charles Elstob, the Prebendary at Canterbury Cathedral.

EIGHTEENTH CENTURY

1702
Anne Stuart, second daughter of James II of England, becomes Queen after her brother-in-law's death.

1703
William Elstob becomes the rector of Saint Swithin's and Saint Mary's in Bothow, London. Elizabeth Elstob joins him there.

1712
Elizabeth Elstob and her brother work together on a copy of the Textus Roffensis.

1714
George of Hanover becomes King of England (the first of his name) after his mother, Sophia, Anne's nearest Protestant relative (James I of England's granddaughter) dies before she can succeed Anne.

1715
William Elstob dies and Elizabeth Elstob's career is at an end.

1717
Elizabeth Carter is born in Deal.

1758
Elizabeth Elstob dies.

Elizabeth Carter publishes the first edition of Epictetus, the proceeds of which will be her principal source of income for the rest of her life. It continues to be the default translation until the 1950s.

1760
George III becomes King of England

1764
James Hargreaves invents the first industrial spinning machine, the Spinning Jenny.

1780
Elizabeth Fry is born in Norfolk, née Elizabeth Gurney.

Between 1780 and 1860 there is an unprecedented migration from villages to the cities– by 1850 c.40% of the population of London has migrated in from outside. Thereafter, the population of the city continues to grow exponentially.

1792
Mary Wolstencroft publishes *A Vindication of the Rights of Woman*.

NINETEENTH CENTURY

1803
Richard Trevithick invents the steam railway locomotive.

1806
Elizabeth Carter dies from an illness contracted 10 years earlier.

1811
Elizabeth Fry is made a minister in the Society of Friends. Two years later she visits Newgate prison.

1818
Elizabeth Fry addresses Parliament on the state of English prisons. She is the first non-royal woman to do so. The 1823 Gaols Act is a direct consequence.

1819
Workmen lowering the road on Folkestone's Dover Hill found numerous skeletons "...about two feet below the surface". An iron spearhead and a sword were found with them. This is the earliest record of the discovery of Anglo-Saxon graves at the site.

1821
Michael Faraday invents the first electric motor.

1828
Harriet Emily Stewart is born.

1833
John Keble's sermon entitled "National Apostasy" is considered the beginning of the Oxford Movement.

During this decade Elizabeth Fry tours the continent, speaking about prison reform.

1837

Charlotte Pearson Boyd is born in Macau. She probably didn't retain any memories of the place, however, since her family almost immediately moves to Brighton.

Victoria (the only child of Princess Victoria of Saxe-Coburg and Edward Duke of Kent, fourth son of George III) becomes Queen of England.

1838

Octavia Hill is born in Wisbech.

1840

Elizabeth Fry establishes a nurses' training school in London in the model of the German Kaiserwerth deaconess house. Florence Nightingale will later take nurses trained by Elizabeth Fry's school to the Crimea.

1841

Frederick Schön leads an expedition down the Niger, with Samuel Crowther. The death-toll is crippling and Frederick concludes that indigenous missionaries need to be cultivated.

1842

Isabella Gilmore is born in London of Emma Morris (née Shelton) and William Morris (no, not that one, the William Morris you've heard of was her brother).

1843

Omoba Aina is born in Oke-Odan to the Yoruba people in Nigeria.

1845

Elizabeth Fry dies from a stroke in Ramsgate, aged 65.

1848

Oke-Odan is invaded and captured by the Dahomeyan army. Aina's parents die during the attack and other residents are either killed or sold into the Atlantic slave trade. Aina is taken to the court of King Ghezo as a slave.

Priscilla Lydia Sellon gathers a community of women around her in a conventual lifestyle and go on to create (in 1856) the Sisters of Mercy in Plymouth.

1850
Captain Frederick E. Forbes of the Royal Navy arrives at the Kingdom of Dahomey on a British diplomatic mission to negotiate an end to Dahomey's participation in the Atlantic slave trade. The mission fails, but Aina is rescued and taken to England, now Sarah Forbes Bonetta.

Charlotte Boyd visits Glastonbury. She later records having knelt in the ruins, solemnly offering herself to "the work of restoration."

The population of London passes two and a half million, approaching four times the size it had been a century ago.

1854
Florence Nightingale travels to the Crimea

1851
Matthew Woodward becomes vicar of Folkestone, aged 26. He finds the church in a state of disrepair but begins a lifetime's work to repair and beautify the church.

1855
Sarah Forbes Bonetta is given into the care of Frederick Schön and his wife at Palm Cottage, Canterbury Road, Gillingham.

1862
Sarah Forbes Bonetta marries Captain James Pinson Labulo Davies at St Nicholas' Church in Brighton, East Sussex. The wedding creates a media storm.

1864
Samuel Crowther is ordained, the first indigenous African bishop of the Anglican Church.

1866
Charlotte Boyd establishes her first orphanage in Kensington.

1868
Joseph Lyne founds the Community of Saints Mary and Scholastica.

Revd Matthew Woodward begins the re-building of the nave of the church, and its re-decoration with the architect R.C. Hussey.

1869
Octavia Hill founds the Charity Organisation Society, an attempt to coordinate the work of several charities.

1875
Charlotte Boyd establishes the English Abbey Restoration Trust.

1877
The Diocese of St Albans is formed. Rochester, Winchester and London are reorganised, leaving a large part of the London slums in the Rochester Diocese.

Octavia Hill founds the Kyrle Society, which forms the basis for the National Trust.

1878
The Community of Saints Mary and Scholastica secedes from Lyne under Abbess Hilda.

1880
Sara Forbes Bonetta dies of tuberculosis on 15 August on Madeira Island, and is buried there (not at sea, as she'd asked).

1882
The Roman Catholic Benedictine monastery at Minster in Thanet is refounded.

Isabella Gilmore is widowed. She trains as a nurse in the tradition brought into England by Elizabeth Fry and recently honed by Florence Nightingale.

1884
Randall Morris, Isabella Gilmore's brother, dies, leaving his eight children (the youngest of which was two years old) in Gilmore's care.

1885
On 17th June workmen 'tenderly' replacing the original Norman wall in the sanctuary of St Eanswythe's Church discover a 'leaden casket' embedded in rubble within the wall. '...within we found some female bones, consisting in the main of the upper portion of the skull, two thigh bones, some fingers and a beautifully white tooth'.

These bones were regarded by many to be Eanswythe's remains.

1886
Isabella Gilmore is recruited by the Bishop of Rochester, Anthony Thorold, to reimagine the role of the deaconess in the Diocese of Rochester.

1887
Charlotte Boyd helps found the Society of John the Baptist, perhaps the first men's community to take proper root in the Church of England.

Isabella Gilmore is ordained deaconess in the Diocese of Rochester.

1891
The Community of the Holy Comforter is founded to undertake the care of the old, the destitute, and children.

Charlotte Boyd buys Malling Abbey.

1893
The community of Saints Mary and Scholastica move into Malling Abbey.

1894
Charlotte Boyd submits to Rome.

1895
Octavia Hill is one of the three founders of the National Trust.

1896
Unable to purchase the ruins of the Abbey at Walsingham, Charlotte Boyd buys the Slipper Chapel, the last of the wayside chapels on the mediaeval pilgrim route, where the shriven pilgrims would remove their shoes before walking the last mile barefoot.

1898
"Adoration of relics in a Parish Church". On 29th September an eyewitness complains to the Times about the practice of exposing the supposed relics of St Eanswythe.

TWENTIETH CENTURY

1901
Queen Victoria dies and Edward VII becomes King.

1906
Mother Hilda Stewart OSB (Order of St Benedict) dies, aged 76.

Charlotte Boyd dies of kidney failure due to diabetes, aged 68, and is buried in an unmarked grave.

Isabella Gilmore retires.

1909
Simone Weil is born in Paris, the daughter of Bernard Weil, a medical doctor, and Salomea Weil; both parents were agnostic Alsatian Jews who move to Paris after the German annexation of Alsace-Lorraine.

1910
George V becomes King, on the death of his brother, Edward VIII.

1911
Abbess Scholastica and the Community of Saints Mary and Scholastica leave Malling Abbey, almost 18 years to the day after they arrived.

1912
Octavia Hill dies, aged 73.

1913
The 'Pantry Nuns' move into Malling Abbey under sister Everilda. Their claim to be the natural successors of the community of Saints Mary and Scholastica is refuted.

1916
The Community of the Holy Comforter moves into Malling Abbey.

1923
Isabella Gilmore dies.

1934
The Slipper Chapel is finally revived as a shrine.

1935
Simone Weil has the first of a series of theophanies, which all take place under the combination of severe migraines and artistic stimulus.

1936
The Spanish civil war breaks out. Simone Weil joins up but is prevented from fighting by her comrades,

who fear her aim is too poor for safety. They are proved right when she shoots a pot of boiling liquid, is severely scalded and has to go home.

1942
Simone Weil's family flees France. She writes *The Need for Roots*, in London, commissioned by General de Gaulle. The following year she is diagnosed with tuberculosis and quickly deteriorates, dying in a sanatorium in Ashford. She is buried in a nearby cemetery.

1952
George VI dies and Elizabeth II becomes queen.

1953
A relic of St Mildred is restored to Minster-in-Thanet.

1962
Charlotte Boyd's grave is marked with a small headstone bearing her name and an iron oblate's cross.

1982
Charlotte Boyd's headstone and cross are moved to Walsingham, to the Slipper Chapel, and a small plaque is left marking her grave.

1987
The first female deacons are ordained in the Church of England.

1990
Excavations ahead of the construction of the Channel Tunnel terminal are carried out by Canterbury Archaeological Trust. These identify mid-Anglo-Saxon occupation at several points close to the source of St Eanswythe's Water, in Folkestone. No sign of her chapel is seen, and the springhead is subsequently buried under the terminal.

1994
Women are ordained as priests for the first time in England.

TWENTY FIRST CENTURY

2002 to 2016
The £5 note commemorates Elizabeth Fry, with her portrait and a (fairly sentimentalised) picture of her visiting Newgate prison.

2007
Canterbury Archaeological Trust excavates a number of deep refuse pits at Henwood, on the Bayle, which produce seventh- to eighth-century pottery and other material culture, including moulds for the production of metal fittings. These pits are probably related to the Minster at Folkestone and indicate its industrial activity.

2014
The Church of England General Synod passes legislation introducing women bishops.

2018-2020
The Finding Eanswythe project establishes that the bones at the Church of St Mary and St Eanswythe, Folkestone, are those of a well-nourished woman, brought up in France, who died in her late teens/early 20s. The casket is comparable to other Kentish coffins from the $8^{th}/9^{th}$ centuries A.D. Radiocarbon dating put the date of death in the second half of the seventh century. Given the lack of other candidates matching the description, whose remains might have been cherished in Folkestone and buried near an altar dedicated to St Eanswythe, the bones were declared to be Eanswythe's mortal remains.

2019
Rose Hudson-Wilkin is consecrated Bishop of Dover.

Glossary

Anabaptist	A break-away Christian group with origins in the 16th century Reformation. Best known for their vigorous disinclination to baptise babies.
Anglo-Saxon	An umbrella term referring to the assortment of Germanic tribes colonising what was to became England.
Augustine (of Canterbury)	The default Augustine in this book: sent by Pope Gregory at the turn of the 6th century to convert the English, inclined to sea-sickness. Started a particular practice of monasticism.
Augustine of Hippo	Crops up occasionally: 4th century African theologian.
Baptism (n), baptismal (adv), baptise (v).	Initiation rite of the Christian Church with various amounts of wetness deployed.
BAME	Black, Asian, Minority Ethnic (now frequently described as Global Majority Heritage)
Bede, Venerable	8th century historian
Benedict of Nursia	6th century pioneer in matters monastic.

Benedictine	Either things in the general spirit of Benedict's (see above) writing, or, more specifically, monastic communities following his rule of life.
Calendar of saints	A formal ecclesiastic list of which people are to be remembered with how much ceremony, when. See also Introduction: note 6
Carolingian Reforms	Series of Church and civic reforms across the 9th & 10th century. See Pioneers: Eadburh.
catholic	Lit. 'universal', which is not intended to be ironic. Both a theological (see below) disposition and a family of churches. Common themes are an enthusiasm for sacraments (below) and veneration of saints (see idolatry) and a more communal way of thinking.
Catholic, Roman, AKA Rome	That Catholic branch of churches that looks to Rome and the Pope.
Christology	lit. 'words about Christ': the study of who Jesus is and what the implications of that might be.
Circa (abbreviated to c.)	Lit. 'around': approximately.
Commemoration	In this book, refers to the hierarchy of festivals in the calendar of saints (see above), being the lowest and humblest remembrance of a person. See also Introduction: note 6
Cranmer, Thomas	16th century theologian and, eventually, Archbishop of Canterbury.

	Wrote a prayer book and much of the liturgical (see below) basis for the Church of England. Reformer.
Eucharist, aka Holy Communion, aka The Mass	That vestigial meal of bread and wine shared between Christian believers which harks back to the last meal that Jesus shared with his disciples.
Gnostic (n & adj)	A family of religions, that may or may not self-describe as Christian, linked by a disparagement of things material and an emphasis on having the right knowledge.
Goscelin	11th century prolific hagiographer (see hagiography).
Gundulf	Not a mighty wizard, but an 11th century Bishop of Rochester.
Hagiography	Lit. 'writings about holy people': stories about the saints, intended to encourage the faithful. Perhaps prone to exaggeration. Written by hagiographers.
Heresy	Heterodox belief considered sufficiently wrong to be dangerous for the health of the Church.
Holy Communion	See Eucharist
Idolatry	The worship of idols, ie of things not God.- the definition is complicated by a somewhat blurry line concerning 'veneration' of saints/statues/sundry items and body parts belonging to saints.

Liminal (adj), liminality (n)	On or across borders, transitional.
Liturgy (n), liturgical (adv)	Liturgy is to worship as water is to fish.
Foxe, John	16th century hagiographer (see hagiography)
Mariolatry	Disparaging term implying that the veneration of the Virgin Mary is in fact idolatry (see above).
Mass	See Eucharist
Minster	The oldest form of monastery in this country, distinct in being much more porous to the community and often being 'double houses', ie housing both men and women.
Non-juror	In this book used regarding those who refused to swear an oath of allegiance to William and Mary.
Office	In this book chiefly used in the specialist sense of daily services of set readings and prayers.
Protestant	Them 'protesting' against Catholicism (see above), usually with themes of personal, informed faith and suspicion of veneration (see idolatry) of saints and sacraments (see below).
Religious, (n & adj)	In this book chiefly used in the specialist sense of things pertaining to vows, monasteries, monks and nuns, but also people who are under monastic vows.

Sacrament	Liturgical (see above) acts that are usually considered to change the nature or state of things, for example Baptism and the Eucharist.
Sacramentalism	In this book, a doctrine specific to Anabaptists and Lollards, rejecting the concept of sacraments.
Theology (n), theological (adj)	Lit. 'words about God': the study of who God is and what the implications of that might be.
Theophany (n)	A manifestation of God, usually in a mystical encounter or experience.
Wergild	Lit. 'human gold': blood money, the compensation for a life.

A reading list of sorts

Most of this book was researched during times of lockdown or partial lockdown during the 2020s Covid-19 pandemic. The vast majority of my reading, therefore, has been gleaned from the Internet. This isn't a comprehensive list, but in case anybody should wish to pick up any of my threads, here are some of my principal sources, listed more or less according to the period they relate to.[1]

Ed. J Doherty, L Hardy, A Richardson and E Williams, *Finding Eanswythe: The Life and Afterlife of a Anglo-Saxon Saint*, (produced by Canterbury Christ Church University: 2020)

Ed. Donald Scrag, *Edgar: King of the English, 959-975* (The Boydell press: 2008)

Ed. Nigel Yates, *Faith and Fabric: a history of Rochester Cathedral 604-1994* (The Boydell Press: 1996)

Louise J Wilkinson, *Eleanor de Montfort: A Rebel Countess in Medieval England* (Continuum Press: 2012

Margaret Gallyon, *The Early Church in Wessex and Mercia* (Terence Dalton Ltd: 1980)

Anthony Marett-Crosby, *The Foundations of Christian England* (Ampleforth Abbey Press: 1997)

Ed. Victoria Blud, Diane Heath and Einata Klafter, *Gender in Medieval Places, Spaces and Thresholds* (University of London: 2019)

Sarah Foot, *Veiled Women: The Disappearance of Nuns from Anglo-Saxon England* vols 1 & 2 (Ashgate Publishing Limited: 2000)

---

[1] It's really not very systematic. Consider it a rebellion, if you will.

Rebecca Moore, *Women in Christian Traditions* (New York University Press: 2015)

Beverley Dee Jacobs, "The Medieval Wall Paintings of Rochester Cathedral" (Rochester Cathedral Research Guild: 2016)

Ed. Helene Scheck and Christine Eadie Kozikowski, *New Readings of Women and Early Medieval English Literature and Culture: Cross Disciplinary Studies in Honour of Helen Damico* (Ark Humanities Press: 2019)

Eric Ives, *The Life and Death of Anne Boleyn* (Blackwell Publishing: 2004)

Diarmaid MacCulloch, *Thomas Cranmer,* (Yale University Press: 1998)

Ed. Jane Chance, *Women Medievalists and the Academy.* (Madison, WI: University of Wisconsin Press: 2005)

Alan Neame, *The Holy Maid of Kent* (Hodder and Stoughton, London: 1971)

Antonia Fraser, *The Weaker Vessel* (Weidenfeld and Nicholson: 1984)

Ed Henrietta Blackmore, *The Beginning of Women's Ministry: The Revival of the Deaconess in 19th-Century Church Of England* (The Boydell Press: 2007)

Janet Grierson, *Isabella Gilmore: Sister to William Morris* (SPCK: 1962)

Owen Chadwick, *The Victorian Church* vol 1&2 (A & C Black Publishers Ltd; 3rd Revised edition: 1971)

Journals of the Rev James Frederick Schön and Mr Samuel Crowther, who, with the sanction of her Majesty's Government, accompanied the Expedition up the Niger, in 1841, on behalf of the Church Missionary Society. With appendices, and a map. (London: 1842)

Montagu Pennington, *Memoirs of the Life of Mrs Elizabeth Carter, With a New Edition of Her Poems, some of which have never appeared before together with her Notes on Bible and Answers to Objections concerning the Christian Religion* (London: 1807)

Jesse Page, *The Black Bishop: Samuel Adjai Crowther* (London:1892)

CH Simkinson *The Life and Work of Bishop Thorold* (Isbister & co: 1896)

The sisters at Malling Abbey very kindly lent me:

Living Stones: The Story of Malling Abbey (Malling Abbey: 2005)

Michael Yelton, *Charlotte Pearson Boyd* (privately printed: 2011)

Dame Eanswythe Edwards OSB, *Saint Eanswythe of Folkestone: Her Life, Her Relics and Her Monastery* (privately printed: undated)

Saint Mildred and her Kinsfolk (privately printed: undated).

I also raided JSTOR pretty comprehensively. Some key articles were:

Priscilla Dorr, "Elizabeth Carter (1717-1806)", *Tulsa studies of women's literature,* (spring: 1986) vol. 5, no. 1

Karen Stöber "Female Patrons of Late Medieval English Monasteries." *Medieval Prosopography,* vol. 31, 2016

Sylvia Federico "The Imaginary Society: Women in 1381." *Journal of British Studies*, vol. 40, no. 2, 2001

Clare Midgley "Can Women Be Missionaries? Envisioning Female Agency in the Early Nineteenth-Century British Empire." *Journal of British Studies,* vol. 45, no. 2, 2006

Diane Watt "Reconstructing the Word: the Political Prophecies of Elizabeth Barton (1506-1534)." *Renaissance Quarterly,* vol. 50, no. 1, 1997, pp. 136–163

Thomas S. Freeman "Research, Rumour and Propaganda: Anne Boleyn in Foxe's 'Book of Martyrs'." *The Historical Journal*, vol. 38, no. 4, 1995

Also, by academia.edu:

Roberta Anderson, "John Foxe's 'seely, poore woman'" (Bath Spa University)

and from era.ed.ac.uk:

Stephanie McGucken, "Saints, Mothers, Personifications: Representations of Womanhood in Late Anglo-Saxon Illustrated Manuscripts" (PhD thesis, University of Edinburgh: 2017)

and from medievalists.net:

Erin Lambert "The Role of Medieval Women as Monastic Patrons" *The Endnote vol 2 (2005)*

from repository.cam.ac.uk:

R. Love (2020) "St Eadburh of Lyminge and her hagiographer" *Analecta Bollandiana*, 137 (II), 313-408.

I owe a lot of my perspective to the following TED talks, which you may also find interesting:

The Danger of a Single Story by Chimamanda Ngozi

How History Erases Women by Bogolo Joy Kenewendo

The Importance of Women's History by Lee Ann Wheeler

Remember the Ladies by Emily Krichbaum

Unlocking the Secret History of Women's Speech by Dana Rubin

There are also a couple of BBC *In Our Time* podcasts that might be of interest:

In Our Time: S23/31 *The Second Barons' War* (May 6 2021)

In Our Time: S16/10 *Pocahontas* (Nov 21 2013)

as well as a short YouTube video by Dr Chris Monk on Elstob's annotation of the Textus Roffensis: *Elizabeth Elstob's Saxon Characters* which you can find via www.themedievalmonk.com/blog

Index

I'm sorry, it was too hard. There were too many Edwards, Hills and Henrys. I suggest you use this page to note any references you want to come back to.

Printed in Great Britain
by Amazon